Proof
Positive

Proof Positive

How to Find Typos and Grammatical Errors Before They Embarrass You

Karen L. Anderson

SkillPath Publications

Mission, KS

Project Editor: Kelly Scanlon

Editor: Jane Doyle Guthrie

Page Layout: Premila Malik Borchardt and Rod Hankins

Cover Design: Rod Hankins

ISBN: 1-57294-043-3

Library of Congress Catalog Card Number: 96-67393

10 9 8 7 6 5 4 3 2 1   96 97 98 99 00

Printed in the United States of America

Dedicated to Betty and Chuck,
my first and best teachers

Contents

Introduction

Nobody notices what proofreaders do until they don't do it! Everyone agrees that proofreading is necessary, yet few can (or will) give it the time and resources it deserves. Good proofreading preserves a writer's or company's professional image by helping present a clear, coherent message. With quality assurance, quality circles, quality control, and improvement being major corporate topics of the day, proofreading takes on a new dimension as a function of quality. Consequently, careless proofreading, whether caused by negligence or ignorance, is even more costly now than a decade ago. The tolls taken in the following examples are enormous.

- In 1988 journalists reported that a major American insurance company paid $11 million to settle a lawsuit out of court. It seems that a company proofreader missed three zeros in the original contract with a huge shipping company. An expensive oversight.

- Historians reported another costly mistake. This one occurred during the final battles of World War II. The Allied forces transmitted a radio frequency to the troops engaged in a maneuver in preparation for D-Day. Regrettably, the frequency was not the intended secret one, but rather a well-known one that the enemy intercepted. More than seven hundred soldiers died. A typographical slip became a fatal error.

- A professional editor and proofreader tells of being hired by a manager who had previously signed a contract for printing a publication with a circulation of four hundred. The editor soon found that her biggest job was on-the-job training for her inexperienced staff. As a result, the first deadline for printing arrived before the first section was complete. The editor decided to submit the material that was prepared, although not proofread, to avoid a large financial penalty. She planned to pay the fee for each required change when the proofs arrived for final approval, relying on that sum being less than the initial penalty would have been. When the proofs seemed overdue, the editor contacted her manager and asked to review the contract. To her horror, she realized that the line specifying proofs was crossed out. The manager had elected to save the additional nominal fee for such a "frivolous" service. The irony in this story is that the manager's photograph appeared in this section of the magazine. Directly under his face, his name was printed as "Mr. Morfart" instead of Mr. Morhart.

Researchers estimate that out of all of the errors that get published, 60 percent result from oversight and 40 percent result from ignorance. Clearly, all the examples mentioned above fall into the first category. The second category can be equally expensive and embarrassing, however. For instance, one writer said that the words "That is now our intention" were proofread with no changes in a letter to a Texas official. Unfortunately, the word "now" should have been "not." The recipient of the letter was offended until the writer explained that a left-handed error on the keyboard caused the miscommunication. The proofreader had failed to check the intent and tone of the letter with the writer.

A typical proofreader on the job is any employee who can read American English and who accepts the duty to proofread documents at work. Few proofreaders even have the word "proofread" in their job descriptions, and even fewer still have training in proofreading skills.

Whether a published error is unnoticed or unknown by a proofreader, it is still an error. Whether the mistake is costly financially or emotionally, it is still costly professionally. The primary task of any proofreader is to find errors before publication. The reality remains: only one guarantee for perfect proofreading exists. Publish! Once a document is released, readers will discover all the remaining errors—actual and imagined. Providing the truths, tools, techniques, and tips needed for a person to become an excellent proofreader is the purpose of this book. Both beginning and practiced proofreaders will find help toward proofreading excellence in the following pages.

1

The Quick Fix:
Ten Fast Answers

Most proofreaders would appreciate fast answers to common concerns. However, most "proofers" also are realistic enough to know that the "quick fix" is limited because American English continuously changes to meet society's needs. The Dictionary Society of America recently reported that only 4 percent of all the words created find their way into a major dictionary. Another source estimates that approximately two thousand new words are added to the language every year.

Not only are new words appearing, but old words are changing in meaning and spelling: *chair* has evolved to include the meaning of a leader of a group, and *database* is now one word. Still another example—many proofreaders have lived through the changes in the way business letters look: the old indented style made way for the block style when early computers were too hard to program for indentations. Now letters carry a variety of acceptable formats. Likewise, changes in punctuation have presented proofreaders with a variety of possibilities: whether to include periods in an acronym, a comma before the word *and* in a simple series, or a comma after the year in a complete date within a sentence. Finally, another example shows how the business world's context demands more language changes with the global vision. For example, does the comma go inside (American style) or outside (British style) the closing quotation mark in a sentence if the readers are international customers? Whew!

When it comes to communicating with language, there are few simple answers. Every effective proofreader must develop common sense, a multimedia center of references, a desire to continue learning, a respect for possibilities and preferences, and a sense of humor. Those are crucial characteristics of a sane and excellent proofreader.

For the developing proofreader, ten crucial questions demand immediate attention:

1. When someone asks to have a document proofread, what does that person expect?

2. How can a proofreader help others understand the different roles of the proofreader and the editor?

3. How can a proofreader prepare to proofread successfully?

4. What references does a proofreader need?

5. When people argue about a language issue, how does a proofreader know what the right answer is?

6. Where will a proofreader find the most errors in a document?

7. How can the proofreader know what the readability level of the document is?

8. What makes communication effective?

9. How can a proofreader do a good job when there is too little time before the deadline?

10. How can a proofreader communicate about the document without putting the writer on the defensive?

Let's look at each of these concerns in detail.

1. When someone asks to have a document proofread, what does that person expect?

What one person expects often is different than what another has in mind. A proofreader does not have to read minds, but must ask this question: "Would you like for me to make corrections only, or would you like for me to suggest improvements as well?"

Proofreading is the final point in the eight-step process for writing:

1. Generate and select ideas.

2. Organize the selected ideas.

3. Draft the document.

4. Take a break.

5. Read the draft aloud.

6. Edit the draft to meet required guidelines in style and strategy.

7. Revise the document, maintaining accuracy and consistency.

8. Proofread to eliminate errors, according to conventions and editorial guidelines.

The Quick Fix: Ten Fast Answers

The proofreader's role here is to check accuracy of content as presented by the writer and consistency of style choices as determined by the editor; consequently, he or she is a liaison between writer and editor. In many busy businesses today, anywhere from one to three or more people can fill these roles in a given situation.

> *Clarify the steps in the preceding list and the roles performed within each to avoid uncomfortable interactions when a writer asks for proofreading services, yet needs or wants editing services instead.*

2. How can a proofreader help others understand the different roles of the proofreader and the editor?

Use this analogy: The writer is like a lawyer representing a case. The editor is the legislator who helps pass the laws that dictate appropriate or inappropriate behaviors and choices. The reader is the judge who will sustain or overrule the writer and the jury who will convict or acquit the writer's point of view. The proofreader is the law enforcement officer who keeps the courtroom orderly and safe according to accepted guidelines and standards. The proofreader's job is to make sure that the writer follows the rules determined by the editor. The proofreader polices the document for any infraction within the accepted and expected code of language conduct. This ensures that communication between the writer and the reader takes place with no distractions and distortions. The proofreader protects the reader and the writer from misunderstandings or confusion. In a sense, the proofreader answers to both the editor and the reader in helping the writer produce the best possible written communication.

If your organization lacks editorial guidelines or a specific style manual, suggest that the team establish a set of language laws that the proofreaders can enforce.

3. How can a proofreader prepare to proofread successfully?

Proofreaders often place themselves in the path of failure by not preparing. Personal, professional, and environmental preparations take only a few minutes of thought. To prepare personally, the proofreader must select his or her peak time of day, eat a light protein-rich meal to stay mentally alert, exercise briefly by taking a brisk walk to the photocopier or going up and down a flight of stairs, and take a few deep breaths to relax the mind.

To prepare professionally, the proofreader will want to consider the following points:

- *Identify all the concerns regarding the assignment.* Know, for instance, if the document has a particular audience with a specific readability level. The general public reads most comfortably at lower readability levels than the typical professional audience. Also, the proofreader must know clearly if the food for thought in this assignment is from an à la carte menu or an all-you-can-eat buffet. Ask questions and get specifications, including an exact day and time that the document you're proofing is needed.

- *Identify team members, time frames, priorities, and other variables.* Team members are essential in excellent proofreading. What one misses, another is likely to see. It only makes sense to have more people review an annual report to the stockholders than a memorandum circulating about the parking lot. Use a dated circulation memo attached to the document that other team members can sign off on. This will make it easier on a proofreader who misses finding an error that is later published. All those who signed the proofreading memo missed the error too. Everyone shares the responsibility and no one person receives the blame.

During weekly team meetings, agree on the priorities of assignments by categorizing A priority documents as "important and urgent," B priority as "important only," and C priority as "urgent only." Then list each category's sequence of documents as 1 for first, 2 for second, 3 for third, and so on. The amount of time spent on the assignment and the number of proofreaders assigned to the document are proportional to the priority level and sequence, with A-1 being the highest priority. If one of the four bosses of an administrative assistant approaches with a new document, the boss and the assistant can decide where it should fall in the sequence of priorities. This often reduces the stress that assistants endure because all the bosses know that success comes from weighing the priorities and that there is only one A-1 project.

- *Clarify any concerns or variables that require someone else's attention.* Great proofreaders often get specifications in writing. They also have "Plan B" ready to go in an emergency if Murphy's Law—"What can go wrong, will go wrong"—takes effect.

- *Schedule proofreading sessions with frequent and regular breaks.* This suggestion includes two overlooked points. First, the reason there is so much "failure" surrounding proofreading is that the deadline for publication or distribution comes before the proofreading is complete, and sometimes before the proofreading has begun! To avoid these last-minute crunches, schedule a conference room for a day or two prior to an important deadline. Invite members of the proofreading team there with different-colored pens—Maureen can use green ink, Drew can use blue, Myrtle can use purple, and Fred can use red. Color coding helps the team identify who is good at punctuation, who specializes in usage, who finds the most style inconsistencies, and who notices formatting details first. Later, when working on urgent documents, each knows who to check with in a hurry for the most likely kinds of errors.

Second, a great proofreader will take mental mini-breaks, perhaps one minute for every fifteen to twenty minutes on task. A fresh, relaxed mind spots more errors than a stale, tense one does. Stand up, stretch, get a drink of water, look out the window—all these quick activities are essential to increasing a proofreader's productivity. This makes sense when you realize that an hour of work with breaks can produce more errors caught than an hour without breaks does. Researchers confirm this.

- *Brainstorm a list of questions about the topic that must be answered in the document.* The most difficult kind of error to locate is one of idea omission. That's because there are fewer clues that something is wrong than other mistakes provide. When a proofreader lists ideas and questions that a reader would expect to have answers to, he or she has a customized checklist for content inclusion and can ask the writer if an idea was omitted on purpose or if it should be added. This is an invaluable service for both the writer and the reader.

To prepare the work environment to better ensure success:

- Create a comfortable workstation, including a footstool. Resting one's feet takes some strain off the back.

- Use correct lighting, preferably incandescent or natural light, to avoid eye strain. Also, use a colored filter over the computer monitor's screen while proofreading from it.

- Assemble references and correcting materials within easy reach.

- Minimize or eliminate visual and audible distractions. Close the door or use a conference room. Ask someone to answer the telephone or switch on voice mail.

> *Take a few minutes to look, listen, and step around your office. Determine what changes would facilitate the proofreading you do, and make them. As a word of caution, give yourself three to four weeks to get used to the changes before judging them unsuccessful. It takes time to operate comfortably within a new world of personal, professional, and environmental preparation.*

4. What references does a proofreader need?

These resources will be helpful to any proofreader:

- A current collegiate-size dictionary (book and software)

- A thesaurus (book and software)

- A calendar

- A calculator

- Client files, telephone directories, and other contact numbers, such as facsimile and electronic mail

- A grammar handbook and software

- An appropriate and current style manual

- The originator and writer of the document

- A proofreading team

- This book!

Using a dictionary copyrighted within the past five years will ensure current usage and spelling. A collegiate-size text or larger will limit the frustration a proofreader feels when a word is missing from smaller volumes. Software thesauruses and spelling checkers are limited in their ability to assist, so back them up with books. It's always best to know more than your computer does in order to make the best language choices (selecting an appropriate homonym, for instance). Be aware that some references are more readable and responsive to the changes in language than others. Typically, Merriam-Webster is liberal and will record alternative usages and spellings earlier than other publishers. Random House's dictionary and thesaurus are moderate choices; Heritage's texts are more conservative. A contemporary usage dictionary is invaluable for showing how a word is used in context—not just what it means. Two excellent such references are Roy Copperud's *American Usage and Style: The Consensus* and S. I. Hayakawa's *Choose the Right Word*. Also, consider a field or industry dictionary, such as medical, legal, or engineering references. A reference librarian will know these resources.

A calendar and a calculator will aid the proofreader in detecting when a day and a date are incompatible and when the sum of the parts doesn't equal 100 percent. Client files and telephone directories will help you check names, addresses, and contact numbers. All of these factors reflect on the credibility of the writer as the reader perceives it. If the writer misspells a customer's name, the latter may assume the writer didn't care enough to get it right. If the wrong fax number appears for the customer's response, the writer is going to look foolish and the company may lose orders. A proofreader who misses these errors loses credibility and looks foolish too.

A self-respecting proofreader will have at least one handbook in addition to a grammar checker in a word processing software package. Without these references, the proofreader is no better off than the writer who is faced with a computer application calling the shots. Computers cannot understand the intricacies of human language. As an example, your software may instruct that "active voice" is the desired usage to create clear, concise writing. But perhaps "passive voice" is a better choice in a particular sentence than "active voice" because the writer either does not know who performed the action or does not want the reader to know who it was. "You made a poor financial decision" may be too direct in most business environments; a better choice may be "A poor decision resulted in lost revenue." A person must decide this, not a computer. The proofreader must discover if the writer is aware of the differences in intent and tone.

Other decisions to prepare for include the forms compiled in a style manual. To maintain consistency within the appointed guidelines, the proofreader must know which style reference to consult. A few common choices include the following:

- American Psychological Association (social sciences)

- Associated Press (journalism)

- University of Chicago (education and business)

- Council of Biological Editors (natural sciences)

- Government Printing Office (U.S. Government agencies)

- Modern Language Association (education and business)

- Gregg (general business)

- Turabian (education)

Ask an editor, librarian, or information specialist to help you select the appropriate one.

The originator and writer can give a proofreader insights about what was intended to be communicated. If the context gives limited information, a proofreader may not know whether *affect* or *effect* is the correct word for the following sentence: "The _____ remains a concern." The sentence could mean the emotion (*affect*) is a concern or the result (*effect*) is a concern. The proofreader has to guess; the writer has the answer. Sometimes, checking with other proofreaders will help you decide what changes are necessary. Certainly a team of proofreaders will find more errors than someone working solo, an excellent reason to create a team if need be. A certain insurance company could have saved $11 million if a proofreading team had reviewed a particular contract.

Finally, keep this book handy. If you've read this far already, there's more that will interest you as you work toward excellence. The last chapter is a gold mine!

Keep these printed references within arm's reach. To be useful, they must be readily accessible—not on the wall at the far end of the office and not in another room. Keep a telephone and fax machine within reach also, to contact the human references you need.

5. When people argue about a language issue, how does a proofreader know what the right answer is?

Frequently people think that what they learned in senior English class is the only correct answer. If Miss Graham said to indent an inch for a new paragraph and to keep two spaces after the sentence period, then it must be right for eternity. Dan Quayle learned to spell "potatoe" in school as a child and was the center of jokes years later because the spelling of the word changed— and no one notified him. The American English language always simplifies and shortens itself as it meets the needs of society. If Americans don't have a need for the silent *e*, they'll drop it— hence, *potato*, *argument*, and *judgment*. (Note that *arguement* and *judgement* are still legitimate British spellings.)

Comparing and contrasting a few examples among three style manuals will help explain the situation. The styles of the Government Printing Office (GPO), the University of Chicago (UC), and the Associated Press (AP) show marked differences in their recommendations for correct and effective written communication:

- *Capitalization preference*

GPO and UC	Kansas State, State of Kansas
AP	Kansas state, state of Kansas
GPO and AP	"The Star-Spangled Banner"
UC	"The Star-spangled Banner"
UC and AP	CST
GPO	c. s. t.

- *Punctuation preference*

GPO and UC	A, B, and C
AP	A, B and C

GPO	the 1990's
UC and AP	the 1990s

GPO, UC, and AP	a well-known person
GPO and UC	a person who is well known
AP	a person who is well-known

- *Syllabication and spelling preference*

GPO and UC	pe-ren-ni-al
AP	per-en-ni-al

UC and AP	ad-ver-bi-al
GPO	ad-verb-i-al

• *Number preference*

GPO

They had many communicators on staff: 10 writers, 7 editors, 14 proofreaders, and 22 speakers.

UC

They had many communicators on staff: ten writers, seven editors, fourteen proofreaders, and twenty-two speakers.

AP

They had many communicators on staff: 10 writers, seven editors, 14 proofreaders and 22 speakers.

Each of these preferences is correct as long as the style remains consistent within the appointed guidelines for a particular document. This demonstration proves why selecting appropriate references for the writing done within a specific business, field, or industry is so important. A proofreader's sanity may depend on these references. Certainly his or her credibility, confidence, and competence do.

> *Check your references before you suggest the writer is wrong or that you are. Perhaps you have another "right" way of constructing the sentence, and perhaps your way is the better way for reasons of consistency or strategy.*

6. Where will a proofreader find the most errors in a document?

Knowing where to look for the most likely errors is about half the job of the proofreader. Researchers have tested hundreds of documents to create this list of hot spots:

• Scan the document for any word that ends in *s*. Errors in case, number agreement, plurals, and possessives thrive around these words.

• Scan the document for punctuation pairs (such as quotation marks and parentheses) and conventions (such as a period at the end of a sentence, correct spacing, and a capital letter at the beginning of the next sentence).

• Errors often happen in clusters. Carefully check around every error for hidden companions.

• Errors often occur at the beginnings and at the ends of documents, when writers and typists are preoccupied.

• If a word has a double letter in its spelling, such as *letter* and *spelling*, check it again. With electronic keyboards, producing the wrong number of the same letter is easy to do. Spell checkers may not catch all the spelling errors, as a major magazine found out when it printed the word *smalller*.

• Common transpositions include *r* and *t*, *t* and *h*, *g* and *h*, *s* and *d*, *b* and *v*, *n* and *m*.

• Common substitutions include *e* and *i*, *d* and *t*, *-s* and *-ed*, *-tion* and *-ing*. Look at the keyboard to see the proximity of the following letters: *s*, *d*, *f*, and *t*. Add an *i* in front of any of these words to get different words: *is*, *id*, *if*, and *it*. Try an *o* with these single letters to get more words: *so*, *do*, *of*, and *to*. Another problem is inadvertently substituting a space or making an omission during word processing: *and* can become *an* or *a* with overzealous pressure on the delete key; *soon* can carelessly become *so on.* The spell checker cannot help here. Check the little words that link thoughts with logic.

• Titles and headings are often overlooked.

• Numbers and their symbols and punctuation frequently hide errors. Check page sequence and enumeration for omissions.

• Capitals for lowercase and lowercase for capitals are confusing. Double-check proper names and creative marketing capitalization and spacing, such as in "WordPerfect."

• Check alignment in format and at margins. Electronic equipment makes it easy to misjudge a space.

• Check the last half of lines that are four inches or longer for disguised mistakes.

• Check the centers of multisyllabic words, where errors often occur.

• Double-check all homonyms for correct spelling and meaning.

• Determine if the sequence or order of information is logical. The progression of events is significant, as the following example illustrates:

Put on the sweatsuit, headband, and jogging shoes; look outside for the weather conditions and see the sleet; go to the refrigerator for cookie dough ice cream.

Putting on the shoes before the sweats could be a problem, and seeing the sleet first would have changed the event entirely. So, the order of presentation does influence the message that the reader constructs during the decoding process.

- Determine if the readability level is appropriate for your intended readers.

> *Knowing where to look for errors will help you get your task done easier and faster.*

7. How can the proofreader know what the readability level of the document is?

If a reader can't read the material comfortably, the writer has wasted time in producing the document. Most grammar checker programs will note the readability level of a document keyed into them. This is helpful. But what happens when the proofreader has only the hard copy, which doesn't contain this information? He or she can turn to a formula: Robert Gunning's Fog Index. Follow the directions below:

1. Count out one hundred words to the end of a sentence (depending on the length of the last sentence you count, this may be a total of 112 words, for instance).

2. Count the number of complete sentences within the designated passage (perhaps there are eight sentences).

3. Count the number of multisyllabic words (those with three or more syllables), omitting the following:

   - Any easy compounds such as *bookkeeper*, which can easily be broken into *book* and *keeper*.

   - Any verbs made from *-ed* and *-ing* affixes, such as *proofreading*.

   - Any proper nouns, such as people's names.

   Maybe there are fifteen legitimate multisyllabic words included in the passage.

4. Divide the total number of words (112) by the number of sentences (8). Calculations: 112/8=14.

5. Add this answer (14) to the number of long words (15). Calculations: 14 + 15 = 29.

6. Multiply this new answer (29) by 0.4, a constant factor. Calculations: 29 x .4 = 11.6. This fictitious sample is written at an 11.6 reading grade level, meaning it falls between the eleventh and twelfth levels.

The general American public is divided into three groups in terms of reading ability: approximately one-fifth are college educated, one-fifth are illiterate, and three-fifths are somewhere in between these extremes. A reading comfort zone suggests that the reader can understand the content in one reading at a fluid pace. Typically, this means that most readers need more white space and a lower reading level to increase immediate comprehension of complex ideas. The general-public comfort zone is the fifth- to eighth-grade levels, as compared with the professional comfort zone of eighth- to eleventh-grade levels. This latter group is made up of people with some advanced or college training. Experts may read familiar technical content at still a higher level, such as the thirteenth level. Consequently, the proofreader who knows that the reading level of a piece is 14.6 can advise the writer that the audience may have to read some sentences more than once.

Overworked readers are less likely to understand the writer's information or to follow his or her position. An excellent business writer wants readers to be enlightened, not exhausted from the experience. Most readers don't have time in a busy workday to be patient with a writer's wordiness or impressive vocabulary, even if they're inclined to be. Because it's unlikely that readers will read a document more than once, the proofreader must assist the writer in making the clearest possible message before the reader receives it.

Given a sample of one hundred words, the following figures become guidelines:

- *Public comfort zone level*—six sentences, four long words; seven sentences, five long words

- *Professional comfort zone level*—five sentences, eight long words; six sentences, ten long words

As the total number of words or multisyllable words increase, so does the reading level. As the number of sentences increases, the reading level decreases. Therefore, to make the reading level more difficult, use longer sentences and words. To make the reading level easier, use shorter sentences and smaller, more common words.

> *A good guideline for sentence length is to consider making a second sentence if the original is twenty-two words long. The average business sentence is ten to fifteen words long. Technical writers frequently allow longer sentences, and many technical readers have a higher threshold for subordination in sentences. However, a general rule to follow limits the number of phrases or clauses in a given sentence to three (four if the original sentence cannot work as two sentences).*

8. What makes communication effective?

What do communicators label the process of conveying the message a sender intends to the receiver? Some think the obvious answer is "communication," yet perhaps this definition better describes a miracle! Professor Albert Mehrabian of the University of California—Los Angeles conducted a significant research study for any student of communication, including proofreaders. He wanted to know what factors make communication effective, and his researchers uncovered three: visual, vocal, and verbal (the last term means the impact of word choices, not just oral communication). The findings stated that how the communication looks determines 55 percent of its effectiveness, followed by 38 percent for how it sounds (read aloud or heard in a reader's imagination), and 7 percent for the actual words and their meanings. This is not to suggest that the verbal factor is the least important just because it has the smallest percentage. What proofreaders must know is that the words themselves influence the reader only after the reader wades through 93 percent of the nonverbal factors first. This means that neatness does count and that readers do judge a book by its cover. Including bulleted lists and boxed notices as visual references offers effective writing devices. This also means that how a document sounds as a proofreader reads it out loud may be a more immediate concern than what the content is. The sound of the transitions from thought to thought and strategic repetitions (such as key words and alliteration) are influential in this component. The content is only effective if the reader stays through the nonverbal components of the communication to experience it.

> *Proofread for visual components such as format and graphics first, vocal components such as flow second, and verbal content last.*

9. How can a proofreader do a good job when there is too little time before the deadline?

A proofreader must first assert a disclaimer if the assignment arrives at the last minute in the final hour. He or she need not accept responsibility for any errors that get published under these circumstances. However, a proofreader must also do the best job possible with the time available. Using the Pareto principle of effective priorities, one can get 80 percent of the results from 20 percent of the effort. Although the best situation would be 100 percent of the results, the proofreader may not have the time to take the best approaches. Here is a **B•E•T•T•E•R** approach for when the best approaches are impossible:

- **B***eginning.* Proofread the beginning of the document—abstract, introduction, first section. Use a magnifying glass to make errors larger than life and, therefore, easier to find fast.

- **E***nd.* Proofread the end of the document—conclusion, recommendations, summary, final section. Use the magnifying tools mentioned above.

- **T***ransitions.* Proofread transitional elements such as the title, headings, and topic sentences. These are areas that readers will read or scan even when they skip the inside paragraphs.

- **T***eam.* Proofread with a team of three. Each person scans or reads the material at least once. Usually, the obvious errors are caught by the cumulative effect.

- **E***levation.* Stand above the document to study the overall view without reading the words. Do this by spreading out all the pages on the floor. Enumeration, pagination, spacing, and formatting errors will be more obvious at this distance. These are the kinds of errors that distract readers.

- **R***ead aloud.* Say and hear errors that are not readily seen. The brain perceives printed material differently orally than it does silently because different parts of the brain process speech than those that process sight. This may be the single best way to proofread when the deadline is now.

> *Many proofreaders believe they are alone in the correction process. This does not have to be the case. Ask co-workers to exchange proofreading favors with you. Ask your boss to arrange a staff or office meeting to discuss the issue of proofreading. Suggest setting up a system of exchange or proofreading teams. As you and others need help fast, the systems are already in place.*

10. How can a proofreader communicate about the document without putting the writer on the defensive?

The proofreader can begin by thanking the writer for trusting him or her with the document. A sincere statement about two or three aspects of the writing that the proofreader especially appreciated comes next. For example, "I like how you use this strategy to get the reader's attention" or "Your content is fascinating; tell me how you became interested in this topic." Suggest that the writer can accept or reject the ideas the proofreader presents as the writer and the editor deem appropriate. This states that the writer is still in control of the choices, which encourages him or her to accept more often than reject the options. Then add these phrases to the dialog:

- "What would happen if you . . . "
- "How about trying this sentence this way . . . "
- "An alternative method is . . . "
- "Would the reader understand this way faster or better . . . "
- "You might write it like this . . . "
- "This is what my reference says . . . What does yours say?"

The Quick Fix: Ten Fast Answers

To avoid coming to blows, check the publishers of the references and choose the appropriate one for the job at hand. If that does not solve the issue, check the copyright year. The most recent year wins this argument.

Take the surgeon's advice: First, do not perform an operation while the patient is watching. In other words, the proofreader can do a swifter job with fewer scars and faster recovery if the writer cannot see the job being performed. Proofreading is a delicate operation that must be handled with a sensitive and a sensible manner. Another suggestion from the surgeon: Patients recover faster when the blood is out of sight, so avoid using red ink unless it's part of team color coding. The red evokes strong emotional responses reminiscent of the days when English teachers butchered a student's essays with critical remarks. Green and purple are safer, gentler colors. Even a pencil can be nonthreatening; it has an eraser on it.

Undoubtedly more questions come to mind. Read on for more answers and practical tips for becoming an excellent proofreader. The next chapter focuses on techniques to use to locate the oversight errors that compose approximately 60 percent of published errors.

2

Mind Tricks: Finding the Oversights

Does your mind ever play tricks on you as you read? Read the following:

Her hand

rested on the

the keyboard.

Now cover up the passage with your nonwriting hand and write the sentence in the space below:

Check what you wrote against what is printed. Does your sample have the same sequence of words? If so, you are unusual. More than 95 percent of people who read a passage with a duplication such as "the the" will register only one occurrence. The brain encounters both and eliminates one as unnecessary, so much so that the brain filters it outside of consciousness. The process resembles becoming unaware of street noise after living on a busy block for a month or not noticing the odor of the stockyards where you work. The brain perceives the stimulus as insignificant, so we're surprised when a visitor points out the honks or the smells. This filtering system is a normal function of the brain, and most proofreaders have normally functioning brains.

No wonder the oversight sneaks past as often as it does. No wonder over half the errors published are of this type. Yet this phenomenon offers an explanation, not an excuse for sloppy proofreading. What happens to many people in the experience that opens this chapter is that they *read* rather than *proofread* the original passage.

Children learning to read learn to focus on the first part of the word just long enough to decode the meaning. As reading becomes easier with practice, mature readers make faster judgments about words and push ahead to grasp clusters of words without consciously deciphering each syllable or letter or space. As a result, readers make worse proofreaders than proofreaders make readers!

Add another factor into the scenario and the plot thickens: Frequently proofreaders must evaluate documents they have composed, typed, or edited themselves. Once the brain knows the main concept, the specific content, the actual intent, and the general context encompassing the text, it reads swiftly to confirm what it already knows. The brain reads what it knows should be there, not necessarily what is there. The reality differs from the perception—people may fail to see the forest for the trees, but the brain fails to see the trees for the forest! When proofreading your own work, you must compensate for this.

The challenge is to trick your brain into consciously registering the error so you will notice it. Professionals share the following tools and techniques to help you become better at this task:

Backwards

Read from the last word in a document to the first word, beginning at the bottom of the last page and moving toward the top of the first page, to find spelling and usage errors. Do the same with sentences—read them in reverse order to spot fragments and run-on sentences. Use this technique with numbers too. Reading each digit of a long sequence in reverse order allows you to spot transpositions, omissions, and additions. This works well with Social Security numbers, telephone and fax numbers, and item numbers.

Centers

Proofreaders who focus their eyes on the middle of words are likely to spot spelling errors that spell checkers and other readers miss. A published typographical error can change "precious children" into "previous children," creating a major distraction and distortion!

Diagonals

Traverse the page by scanning for the first word at the top left and jumping across the line to the last word at the top right. Then jump down one line and across to the left margin, read the word and move to the right. Proceed in a zigzag pattern to identify redundancies, duplications, and other problems that often occur at the beginning or the end of a line. This technique is useful for tracking hyphenations. A typical guideline is no more than three end-of-line word divisions in a row (and sparingly overall).

Hard Copy

Print a copy to proofread rather than reading exclusively at the computer screen. Photocopies are especially good because the print is slightly raised from the page. Your brain perceives the depth of this print easily, noticing errors more readily on paper than on screen.

Inside Out

A proofreader can hold a single-sided copy up to the light with the print facing away from view. An experienced eye can locate words that seem to make sense, such as *no* for *on*. Other little words to check are those that compose approximately 25 percent of the language use: *I, you, the, a, to, is, it, that, of, and,* and *in*. Misplaced formatting and mismeasured kerning may also be obvious with this technique.

Sideways

Turn the hard copy to its side with the right margin pointing upward. Hyphenations and leading stand out. Delete any distractions.

Tilt

Move the top of the document downward as the bottom remains stationary. Stop the descent of the top when blocks of copy seem to squeeze the white spaces among sections. Leading and alignment problems show up this way.

Upside Down

Spot capitalization confusions by looking at the page bottom-side up.

Leap

Glance from one heading to the next as if your eyes were a pebble skipping across water. Scan this way for punctuation pairs, proper nouns, numbers, and type attributes.

Blow Up

Enlarge the printout to about twice the original size (either a magnifying tool or a photocopier will work). Blow up the white space between lines by double or triple spacing. The white space draws attention to mistakes.

Out Loud

Read the content out loud or listen to someone else read it. This technique gives your mistakes a voice—and you can literally hear them. You can also use an audiotape recorder to read into and then play back as you check the text on paper.

Dueling Partners

One proofing partner reads aloud as the other follows silently with a second copy or the original. Take turns in each position.

Line Drawings

Construct a diagram of a difficult sentence. Remove the words and focus on the concept of the sentence to determine structure, logic, and punctuation. For example, to analyze "We will discuss national

reports, performance criteria, and satellite training," use a vertical line for the capital letter and insert punctuation and cue words:
|_____, _____, and _____. This is the design of a sentence with a simple series of three items listed and set apart by commas.

Focus Frame

Cut a window into a sheet of cardboard. The frame acts as a visual shield that focuses your attention inside the window. The size of the window can vary from one line or column to several. After an interruption such as a telephone call, you can get back to work faster by zeroing in on the area that is framed.

Slant Board

Use a lap or a desk board that stands as an easel would. On it place two to three pages in a column. Formatting and highlighting are easy to track this way.

Colored Paper

Print a document that has evolved through several versions on a different color of paper each time. For example, use pale blue for one version and yellow for a subsequent revision. Mistakes will show up like bruises.

Ruler

Use a straight edge to move down the page, line by line. Then move the ruler up the page. Next move it across the page from right to left, and from left to right. Notice alignment and spacing as you go.

Imaginary Columns

Use a long straw or slender dowel rod to make a phantom vertical alley through the text. Scan the right column for anything out of the ordinary. Because each sentence is interrupted, it's less likely you'll get involved with the content and more likely you'll find oversights. Then scan the left column.

Colored Highlighters

Check all titles, headings, subheadings, type attributes, and format specifications by color coding them, scanning for one kind at a time.

Colored Pens

Teams can color-code among themselves, or a single proofreader may use one color to check punctuation and capitalization, one for spelling and usage, and one for grammar. Or, the proofreader may use one color to communicate with the writer, another to communicate with the editor, and a third to correct errors.

No one of these ideas is better than another—all are useful at various times and with a variety of documents. Test them and add them to your repertoire when you find a good fit. Using combinations of these tools and techniques will bring you proofreading success in finding the errors that slip past others.

In the next chapter, the mysteries of grammar unfold in a review of the basics.

3

The Movie Director: Grammar Basics

Forty percent of errors published result from writers and proofreaders not knowing that a construction they read was wrong. Periodically reviewing basic grammar can refresh your understanding of how our language performs. You can compare it to making movies.

The movie director positions the actors and the props so that the action on the screen makes sense to the audience. The director uses film-making techniques such as facing the characters toward the camera and using the audience's native language for the dialog in the story. As we direct verbal and nonverbal language components, we're focusing a message for our audience much like a movie maker does. We think, speak, and write according to grammatical forms.

Grammar pertains to how words are positioned (syntax) so they make sense (morphology). People know a lot about the grammar of their native language by the time they are only two or three years old. Children first begin to arrange words into elementary sentences—into frames of thought—such as these:

Me with!   Chris got ouchy.

You falled.   Baby sleep.

Each of these sentences follows patterns of grammar. Despite the inaccuracies of flawed diction and usage, within the examples are typical subject-verb (actor-action) order and small units of meaning (morphemes) such as *-ed* for past tense and *-y* for description. Impressive observation, direction, action, and conviction are also evident in these examples. Certainly the communication of children is meaningful, although general and immature, much like a student movie. Communicating in the quality of a four-star film comes later.

Imagine a scene from a movie about beings from another galaxy who speak a language with grammar similar to American English, although the actual words are different. You will recognize parts of the nonsense words below:

Thutly, Halya en dawing ro fle unreplokasive zorgation.

Chances are you identified *T-, -ly, -ing, un-, -ive,* and *-tion* as similar to American English. These morphemes have recognizable and grammatical functions, and each helps set the stage in the sentence. To illustrate this for yourself, answer the following sentences:

- What word acts as an introduction for the sentence?

  _____

- What word names the "actor" in the sentence?

  _____

- What words represent the action in the sentence?

  _____

- When is this action taking place?

  _____

- What word shows a relationship?

  _____

- What words describe something in the sentence?

  _____

- What is the thing being described?

  _____

This nonsense script seems vaguely familiar because you would use this same construction to say, "Fortunately, I am moving beyond the unreceptive position."

As a child, you could easily process grammatical patterns simply by noting positions and units of meaning. Therefore, you could say "womans" to mean "more than one woman" and "you runs" to mean "one person besides me is running." Even if you could not explain it, you noticed that an *s* at the end of a noun made the word plural and an *s* at the end of a verb made the word fit a singular actor.

Parts of Speech

Identifying the parts of speech and the parts of a sentence can generally help grammar seem more logical. This section provides some "mind hooks" for remembering the eight parts of speech that describe the common roles words have. The highlights will help you focus on visual clues and notice significant morphemes.

Noun: Name of a person (actor: *Terry*), place (setting: *Kansas City*), thing (prop: *computer*), animal (character: *Alaskan malamute*), or idea (time or thought: *noon, mood*). Associate the *N*'s in *name* and *noun*. Examples of typical noun morphemes are found in *nation, nomenclature, toys, occasion, management, author, economist, celebrity, sexism, defendant,* and *excellence.*

Pronoun: A "professional" substitute for a noun, a kind of understudy that replaces an exact person's or thing's name. Examples include *I, you, us, it, this, anyone, somebody, themselves, few,* and *many.*

Verb: Expresses existence (a state of being) or behavior (action). Examples of verbs are *to be, to have, to run, to act,* and *to view.* Common endings are found in *runs* (third-person singular present tense), *acted* (regular past participle), and *viewing* (present participle).

Adverb: An advertisement that adds information about a verb, an adverb, or an adjective; sometimes called a "modifier" or a "descriptor." Examples include *not, too, very, really, easily, usually,* *generally, hungrily,* and *honestly.* The most common adverb morpheme is *-ly.* Adverbs often direct intensity and quality.

Adjective: An advertisement that adds information about a noun or a pronoun; sometimes called a "modifier" or "descriptor" like the adverb. Examples are *tentative, casual, noisy, shrinkable, realistic,* and *instantaneous.* Adjectives often note quantity and identity.

Preposition: A word that relates position or the relationship between and among ideas or images in a sentence. Examples include *under, over, before, for, to, at, with, of, beside, behind, among, between, at, toward, inside, on, in,* and *by.* Prepositions provide "stage directions."

Conjunction: A word that represents the junction of things or people or ideas. *And, or, but, because,* and *nor* provide the most common links. They're sometimes called connectors.

Interjection: A spontaneous emotional expression, such as how you feel when getting an injection. Examples include *Well, Oh no!, Um, Not so!,* and *Ouch!* A comma or an exclamation point sometimes follows an interjection.

Parts of a Sentence

If you imagine the eight different roles that words perform in speech as resembling the primary roles an actor performs (hero, villain, etc.), then you can see that just as the performer adapts secondary roles and styles to develop his part into a character, words too develop secondary roles called the parts of a sentence. This section will show how the position of a word has a decided impact on the development of a sentence.

Two main parts of a sentence are the *complete subject* and the *complete verb* or *predicate*. The complete subject names the actor or prop that does something. Usually the complete subject appears early in the sentence. The complete verb or predicate usually follows the subject and always contains the main behavior (action) or existence (state of being). Even toddlers create sentences with these two parts. Read the following sentence:

> *Many people watch old movies on late-night television while they wait for sleep.*

The complete subject consists of *Many people*. *People* is the simple subject, and *Many* is the modifier that completes it. The complete predicate consists of the simple predicate, *watch*, and the words that follow it—*old movies on late-night television while they wait for sleep*.

When a group of words has only a noun form or a verb form, but not both, it is a *phrase*. In the sample sentence, *on late-night television* and *for sleep* are phrases that include nouns and no verbs. Each begins with a preposition, so each is a prepositional phrase. Rearranging the sentence produces another kind of phrase:

> *Lying on their beds, many people watch old movies on late-night television.*

Lying on their beds is a participial phrase because it begins with that particular verb form (*lying*)—a participle. The verb form lacks the clearly stated subject. In fact, prior to the comma and the independent clause, the audience (the reader) is blind to which actors are involved. Both dependent clauses and phrases are incomplete thoughts. They act as crew members that serve the cast, represented by the independent clause of the sentence.

Kinds of Sentences

Film directors use different camera techniques to create and keep interest. For example, a zoom focuses on one simple idea or image, a split screen helps express two concurrent or compound events, and an overhead shot may show a complex plot unraveling.

The writer creates and keeps interest in a similar way by arranging sentence patterns. The simple sentence consists of a base clause with one or more phrases sometimes attached. Combining different sentence patterns and mixing them with a variety of clauses and phrases produce the other, more complicated kinds of sentences. Look at the examples below to see the combinations that make up the four basic kinds of sentences:

Simple: Actors read parts for directors each day. (one independent clause)

Compound: All actors read parts, and some actors circulate portfolios. (two independent clauses)

Complex: After an actor circulates a portfolio, he may read for a part. (one dependent clause, one independent clause)

Compound-Complex: Before an actor gets a part, she must rehearse for the audition and she must read the part well. (one dependent clause, two independent clauses)

Five Essential Laws of Grammar

More than five hundred grammar rules exist, yet writers and proofreaders need to know only five general ones to construct a movie for the reader:

1. Emphasize at the beginning and the end.

2. Keep all parts that describe something in a sentence as close as possible to that something.

3. Make sure language agrees in number and reference.

4. Limit phrases and clauses to no more than three for complex content and four for simple content.

5. Be consistent in style and content.

When a proofreader allows a writer to violate any of these five guidelines, the reader will lose the story line and mentally "walk out" of the movie! For example, the first two laws are violated in this published goof: "The Mercy Center will offer a support program for women whose husbands have died next Tuesday."

The Mercy Center and *Tuesday* have the power positions in the sentence—beginning and end. Although obviously it's the program that will run next Tuesday, as written the juxtaposition of *husbands* and the day suggests other plans for Tuesday. If the sentence is rewritten as "The Mercy Center will offer a support program next Tuesday for women whose husbands have died," then *the Mercy Center* and *died* assume the power positions. If "Next Tuesday the Mercy Center will offer a support program for women whose husbands have died," then the focus shifts to the day.

The third law is violated in the following sample written to an insurance company as part of a claim: "I drove my truck into the bridge and it didn't fit." *It* here is a vague pronoun with a grammatical reference to *bridge* as the last possible reference in the sentence. Yet of course it was the truck that did not fit the bridge.

The fourth law is stretched in this sentence: "The proofreaders drank coffee while the movie critics wrote scathing reviews on their laptop computers about the unconvincing characters within the context of the first three hours of the production." Two clauses and five phrases later, not even a dedicated proofreader cares to untangle the mess.

The fifth law states that style and content must have consistency. An example: "We will collect $13 from each member, totaling two dollars for snacks and 9 dollars for a group gift." The varied number style could make the best proofreader scream, and the inaccurate sum would bring an accountant to tears.

Seven Deadly Sentence Sins

Infractions against the Five Essential Laws of Grammar frequently can be characterized by one of the following seven deadly sentence sins:

1. The sentence fragment

Example: "Before finishing the assignment." (violates law 1)

Solution: Complete the sentence with an independent clause.

Explanation: A sentence fragment is usually an afterthought written as a separate sentence.

> *You can identify the sentence fragment by reading the sentences of a document in reverse order, from the end of the document to the beginning. Correcting the fragment is often a simple matter of inserting it into the end of the sentence that came before it.*

2. The run-on or fused sentence

Example: "Our overhead has doubled this year our assets have tripled." (violates laws 4 and 5)

Solution: Begin a new sentence with "Our assets . . . "

Explanation: Two sentences are brought together without a transitional word or punctuation mark.

> *Use the following guide for long sentences: If there are twenty-two or more words, consider breaking it into more than one sentence.*

3. The comma-splice sentence

Example: "Chris and Taylor will present their report, we'll hear it at the board meeting." (violates laws 4 and 5)

Solution: Replace the comma with a semicolon to divide the two sentences, or add *and* after the comma.

Explanation: Two complete sentences are joined with a comma. To correct this kind of sentence error, add a conjunction such as *for, and, nor, but, or, yet,* or *so* after the comma, or change the comma to a semicolon.

> *The first letters of these common conjunctions spell a nonsense word that is easy to remember:* fanboys.

4. Subject-verb nonagreement

Example: "The Board of Directors, advised by the actuaries, make the final decision." (violates law 3)

Solution: Since *Board* is the subject, *makes* should be the matching singular verb.

> *Often a simple subject is followed by a prepositional phrase and then the predicate. Remove the phrase to bring the subject closer to the verb to see and hear the correct subject-verb combination.*

5. Pronoun reference problem

Example: "Everyone will ensure their employees a paid vacation." (violates laws 2 and 3)

Solution: Change *Everyone* to *Employers* to match the plural form of *their.*

> *Learn the WITTY words:* who *and* whom*; it *and* its; they, them, *and* their*; thing *and its compounds, and* you. *These words typically cause reference problems. Check each one carefully for a clear, direct connection to the word it stands for.*

The Movie Director: Grammar Basics

6. Misplaced modifier

Example: "Explaining the accident, the cow crossed in front of the car." (violates laws 2 and 3)

Solution: The cow did not explain, so state who did directly after the comma.

> *When a sentence begins with a word ending in* -ing, *it is probably the beginning of a participial phrase. These phrases commonly modify the subject. That subject must appear after the phrase's comma.*

7. Nonparallelism

Example: "Remember to be assertive, creative, organized, and focusing on selling to the customer." (violates laws 3 and 5)

Solution: Use adjective forms for all the modifiers, including *focused.*

Explanation: Nonparallelism refers to a missed opportunity to compose a sentence with "parallel" parts. Forming words or phrases in similar ways shows the reader that the parts have equal weight in the sentence. This technique may show coordination or correlation.

Parallelism uses the repetition of words, sounds, or parts of speech to convey the equality of two or three components. Notice in the previous example that the adjective suffixes -ive and -ed are part of the four descriptive words. Other examples of parallelism: "The first answer is . . . and the second is . . . ," "Drinking and driving can be deadly," "The assistant is both competent and independent."

Simply put, grammar is how words are combined to create meaning. As writers communicate, they engage the brains of their audience to process their own thinking and they invite that audience to respond. As the next chapter will illustrate, punctuation marks act as cues that help the audience interpret the intended message. In that sense, punctuation serves as the gestures and inflections of the silent sentence. Their delivery is the domain of the proofreader and a good writer.

4

Brain Scripts: A Punctuation Review

Movie directors rely on the scriptwriter's stage directions just as a reader relies on punctuation to interpret the image and message of the storyline or sentence. For example, does a new president say, " . . . so help me God" or "So . . . help me, God"? The punctuation provides the cues. The proofreader must know how to move among these marks with agility and confidence, as if he or she were maneuvering a vehicle around an obstacle course, as simple punctuation can significantly change the meaning of a sentence. Compare "A woman without her man is nothing" to "A woman: without her, man is nothing"—the same words send two very different messages because of the signals the punctuation waves in front of the reader.

Functions of Common Punctuation Marks

Following are brief overviews of the punctuation business people encounter every day in typical documents generated in the workplace.

Period (.)

Use the period at the end of a sentence that declares something or makes a statement. Some style guides also call for the period to appear in certain abbreviations, such as U.S., a.m., St., and so on. Three spaced periods used to indicate omitted material at the beginning of a sentence or inside a sentence are called *ellipsis marks*. If these marks are used at the end of a sentence, four periods are needed.

Question Mark (?)

The question mark applies when a sentence is intended as a question, even if the question appears in the form of a declarative statement.

Exclamation Point (!)

Use the exclamation point sparingly: No more than one to a memorandum, and never more than one at a time. "!!!!!!!!" is a sure sign of an amateur writer and proofreader. Save the sign for a surprise that the reader would not otherwise notice through the words and imagery of the sentence.

Comma (,)

The comma is the most common punctuation mark after the period. No wonder so many writers and proofreaders look dazed after a heated argument over where to place one. Line drawings that illustrate the three functions of the comma can relieve the proofreader from the burden of memorizing comma rules.

Separate

| *_____ A, B, and C.   (simple series)

|_____ A-1, A-2; B-1, B-2; and C. (complex series)

|_____, and _____. (compound sentence)

Isolate

|_____, Zack, _____ (direct address or appositive that interrupts the sentence without changing its meaning)

*This symbol (|) indicates a capital letter at the beginning of a sentence.

Accommodate

Well, _____. (a calm interjection announces the sentence without an immediate exclamation point)

If _____, then _____. (a complex sentence where the dependent clause introduces the independent clause)

I_____; consequently, _____. (compound sentence where an adverbial conjunction introduces an independent clause)

However, _____. Being efficient, _____. (a simple sentence where an adverb or phrase introduces the clause)

The typical transitional words in this construction are multisyllabic, unlike the "fanboys." These words include likewise, accordingly, therefore, consequently, *and* however *(the first letter of each creates the acronym LATCH). A note of caution:* However *can interrupt a single sentence or add to one of the independent clauses in a compound sentence. The first requires commas around* however, *and the second may require a semicolon in front of and a comma after the word.*

Semicolon (;)

Two rules apply to the semicolon—use it to divide two independent clauses in a compound sentence, and use it in partnership with commas in a complex series.

Colon (:)

Use the colon with a heading or an independent clause that introduces an explanation or an example. Do not use one after a sentence fragment, such as "The items you should bring to the meeting are: your budget, your schedule, and your goals for next quarter." The example could have the series of items after a heading and the colon, however ("The items: . . . "), or after a complete sentence ("Bring these items with you to the meeting: . . . ").

Dashes and Hyphen (—, –, -)

The em dash (—) shows interruption in a quotation or a dramatic pause.

The en dash (–), slightly shorter than the em, is used with numbers, such as in ranges of dates and page numbers, and also to hyphenate open compound adjectives such as New York–style.

The hyphen (-) connects compound words and divides syllables.

Three prefixes that require the hyphen are all- (all-American), ex- (ex-president), and self- (self-esteem).

Parentheses, Brackets, and Braces (( ), [ ], and { })

Parentheses appropriately enclose material assumed to be extra information that is nonessential for the meaning of a sentence. Further, a definition may be inserted behind a word for the reader's convenience, or the abbreviation of an organization may be included for easy reference later.

Brackets flag editorial changes in a quotation that increase readability or designate an original error such as a misspelled name (place "[*sic*]" after the error).

Although braces as punctuation rarely show up in standard nontechnical documents, they are used when two levels of bracketed information are embedded within a third. Watch for them in technical writing that contains mathematical equations and avoid them in business writing.

Apostrophe (')

Apostrophes have two main functions that do not vary between style manuals: they're used to form contractions (we'll, couldn't) and to create many possessive nouns and some pronouns. Further, some style manuals prefer that you use an apostrophe to form the plurals of numbers and letters (1's, B's).

> *Use the "of test" to know whether an apostrophe is needed. For example, using the "of test," reword "the manager's office" to determine whether you are correctly using an apostrophe. "The office of the manager" tells you that the form is possessive and thus requires an apostrophe.*

Quotation Marks (" " and ' ')

Use double quotes for dialogue, for titles of short literature published inside a larger piece (an article in a journal, a cartoon in a newspaper, a chapter in a book, a section in a long report), and to set off slang or other examples of irony or uncommon usage. Certain sciences also allow writers to highlight terms with double quotation marks.

Single quotes serve for quotations or literature titles inside quotations. These can also be used to highlight terms in linguistics and philosophy.

The British style often shows the single quotation marks being used first with the double as the inside marks when a quote is stated within a quote. Proofreaders will commonly see this style in international communications.

In the American style, commas and periods always go inside the closing quotation mark, whereas semicolons and colons go outside. The question mark and the exclamation point go inside if they belong to the quote itself; they're placed outside if they belong to the commentary outside the quote. When the single and the double quotation marks end at the same time, the American style shows the period, the closing single mark, and the closing double mark like this: .'" (An interesting note: *Newsweek* magazine editors place the period between the single and the double marks.)

Each nonverbal mark carries its own message to the reader's brain. Each mark has an influence on what the reader sees on the screen of his or her mind while reading the script created by the writer and proofreader. The following exercise gives you an opportunity to hone your punctuation skills. Give it a try before moving to the next chapter, which considers what can happen when poor speaking habits signal written disasters.

Punctuation Practice

Punctuate the following sentences appropriately.

1. Punctuation marks show the readers brains how to process groups of words into meaningful images

2. What punctuation frustrates you

3. Yes I agree

4. Morgan please send me a copy of our annual report that the printers have now

5. The colon commands one requirement it is known as the power mark

6. The semicolon has two basic rules for its use one as a soft period one as a hard comma

7. Call me any time even late at night

8. My facsimile number is 913 888 1234

9. Our two week vacation begins at the end of October which is when the front office celebrates our departure with a Halloween party

10. Dr. Teaberry a research scientisst *sic* fed data into the computer the assistant recorded into the minutes of the committee meeting on January 31 1995 last Thursday

11. Some people just cant seem to grasp the concept that the apostrophes function is like that of a flag either a symbol of ownership or loss

12. Please insert this title into the library records MNOPs Marketing Report for 1995

13. Its your turn to use the conference room

14. I wonder if were ready to vote on the proposal yet

15. Begin making arrangements for the office party ie Kims promotion to president and invite honored guests eg Kim and members of the board

16. To show the reader that some words are left out of the quotation at the beginning or inside the quoted information the writer will use elipses this way of the people by the people the writer will use this punctuation mark this way at the end of a sentence so help me God

Punctuation Practice Answers:

1. Punctuation marks show the readers' brains how to process groups of words into meaningful images.

2. What punctuation frustrates you?

3. Yes, I agree.

4. Morgan, please send me a copy of our annual report that the printers have now.

5. The colon commands one requirement; it is known as the power mark.

6. The semicolon has two basic rules for its use: one as a soft period, one as a hard comma.

7. Call me any time, even late at night.

8. My facsimile number is 913-888-1234.

9. Our two-week vacation begins at the end of October, which is when the front office celebrates our departure with a Halloween party.

10. "Dr. Teaberry, a research scientist [*sic*], fed data into the computer," the assistant recorded into the minutes of the committee meeting on January 31, 1995, last Thursday.

11. Some people just can't seem to grasp the concept that the apostrophe's function is like that of a flag: either a symbol of ownership or loss. (colon could be a dash or comma instead)

12. Please insert this title into the library records: "MNOP's Marketing Report for 1995."

13. It's your turn to use the conference room.

14. I wonder if we're ready to vote on the proposal yet.

15. Begin making arrangements for the office party (i.e., Kim's promotion to president), and invite honored guests (e.g., Kim and members of the board).

16. To show the reader that some words are left out of the quotation at the beginning or inside the quoted information, the writer will use elipses this way: " . . . of the people, by the people . . . "; the writer will use this punctuation mark this way at the end of a sentence: "so help me, God . . . ".

Punctuation Practice II

Here are some additional sentences to punctuate.

1. The boss is pleased he has always liked creative responses to problems

2. I like discussions the supervisor decisions

3. The on switch had a horrifying meaning he had been electrocuted

4. The United States has a government of the people by the people for the people

5. His ambition and competence his creativity and production his gentleness and understanding make him a respected co worker

6. All the scholarly disciplines and especially all the sciences physical biological social share the burden of searching for truth

7. Since she has imagination since she has talent since she has experience she will be hired

8. Every writer must obey what someone called the Platinum Rule the rule not to confuse the reader

9. The manager must remember one main point employees can only do what they have time to do

10. A minute scratch of ink etching like wind upon a cliff can make millions think

11. Determined to succeed the project coordinator wrote a third draft

12. Frantically the safety inspector called for help

13. Despite a masters degree in economics the only position Terry could get was making change in a casino

14. The managers duties include supervision and evaluation training and coaching cost analysis and cost effectiveness

15. Chris Scott and Jan all will receive certificates of recognition

16. Will you

17. The more I write the more I appreciate word processing

18. The first stage is the most difficult to complete and the last stage is the easiest to finish

19. Formatted the diskette still did not work

20. Emphasize your point by using a creative sentence pattern to seize the readers attention

Punctuation Practice II
Answers:

1. The boss is pleased: he has always liked creative responses to problems.

2. I like discussions; the supervisor, decisions.

3. The on-switch had a horrifying meaning: he had been electrocuted.

4. The United States has a government of the people, by the people, for the people.

5. His ambition and competence, his creativity and production, his gentleness and understanding make him a respected co-worker.

6. All the scholarly disciplines and especially all the sciences—physical, biological, social—share the burden of searching for truth.

7. Since she has imagination, since she has talent, since she has experience, she will be hired.

8. Every writer must obey what someone called the "Platinum Rule," the rule not to confuse the reader. (comma could be a colon or em dash instead)

9. The manager must remember one main point: employees can only do what they have time to do.

10. A minute scratch of ink, etching like wind upon a cliff, can make millions think.

11. Determined to succeed, the project coordinator wrote a third draft.

12. Frantically, the safety inspector called for help.

13. Despite a master's degree in economics, the only position Terry could get was making change in a casino.

14. The manager's duties include supervision and evaluation, training and coaching, cost analysis and cost effectiveness. (*manager's* for one manager and *managers'* for more than one)

15. Chris, Scott, and Jan—all will receive certificates of recognition.

16. Will you?

17. The more I write, the more I appreciate word processing,

18. The first stage is the most difficult to complete, and the last stage is the easiest to finish.

19. Formatted, the diskette still did not work.

20. Emphasize your point by using a creative sentence pattern to seize the reader's attention. (could be *readers'* for more than one reader)

5

Averting Disasters: Keeping Spoken Usage Errors Out of Print

Bad habits and poor choices can cause havoc in the delicate environment of the business sentence. One slip can cause a tornado in a relationship or a volcano in the office. The writer and the proofreader must know the conditions in and around a document as well as a meteorologist must know the weather conditions to give a report.

The early search-and-rescue techniques described in Chapter 2 will help defer some of these "natural disasters," yet some occur because the proofreader thought the sentence sounded "right" and looked correct. But errors that the ear will often forgive are simply unacceptable in writing. This chapter is about heading off some of those toxic tides.

Bad Habits

The proficient proofreader can find all the errors in the sentences below:

- We was seniors together in 1990.

- The printer is not even broke.

- I wish we could of went to the annual conference.

- So write natural for your reader.

- Take the assignment slow.

- The supervisor said they use to do it that way.

- Me and them will meet you there at 10:15 tomorrow morning. They's coming down the hall now.

- Yes, this is me speaking.

- Are you suppose to pronounce it like that?

Verbs, adverbs, and pronouns are especially vulnerable in the spoken grammar that bombards our language today. Each of the preceding statements has found its way into the American business community. But such grammar lapses can cause lost esteem and credibility.

In the samples listed above, the original speakers often omitted the suffix of the past participle or the adverb. The *d* sound in *used* and *supposed* gets lost in the pronunciation of the *t* sound in *to* that immediately follows. The contraction *could've* is pronounced like "could of" so often that many proofreaders miss this error. These examples are evidence that good grammar references are still necessary, despite what the spelling and grammar checkers know!

The proficient proofreader found all these bad habits in the sentences on the previous page:

- We were seniors together in 1990.

- The printer is not even broken.

- I wish we could have gone to the annual conference.

- So write naturally for your reader.

- Take the assignment slowly.

- The supervisor said they used to do it that way.

- We will meet you there at 10:15 tomorrow morning. They're coming down the hall now.

- Yes, this is I. (or, Yes, this is _____ (name) _____.)

- Are you supposed to pronounce it like that?

Another area of concern involves poor choices.

Poor Choices

Many written usage errors are simply tied to poor pronunciation and bad spoken grammar. Words such as *affect* and *effect* are pronounced similarly but spelled and used differently. Attending to speech and diction will help proofreaders catch some of the 40 percent of errors they may not have noticed previously.

Usage errors can become even worse if common English words, used differently by Americans and the British, are confused. A few examples will illustrate this. In Great Britain the hood of a car is its *bonnet* and the roof is its *hood*. The *boot* is the car's trunk. Obviously, therefore, "Please look under the hood and remove the boot" will have two different meanings for garage crews in various English-speaking countries. In America, a person traveling might say, "Please give me a wake-up call in the morning," while those in England might say, "Please knock me up in the morning."

> The *"Commonly Misused Words"* list in Appendix C gives more information about these potential usage disasters. The proofreader will find rescue information in it and in a good grammar handbook. Looking up each issue as it faces you, day by day, is the best way to learn all these usage conditions.

Excellent writers and proofreaders know the differences among the following usage dilemmas. From the choices given, select the word or phrase that best reflects the sentence's meaning:

1. The writer asks how the document will _____ the reader. **(affect, effect)**

2. Careless errors _____ most readers. **(aggravate, annoy)**

3. I like my style manual better _____ yours. **(than, then)**

4. We are _____ to present this project. **(anxious, eager)**

5. Please _____ your readers that you meant well. **(assure, ensure, insure)**

6. What _____ of the budget does your department need? **(percent, percentage)**

7. The copier _____ ran out of paper. **(continually, continuously)**

8. Be prepared to discuss items _____ budgets and markets. **(like, such as)**

9. If the writer merely _____ the facts, the reader may be confused. **(infers, implies)**

10. Receiving has processed _____ units this week than last week. **(fewer, less)**

11. We heard about _____ getting certified. **(Terry, Terry's)**

12. Be sure _____ discuss our plan with your crew. **(and, to)**

13. This printer performs _____ than our previous one did. **(more smoothly, smoother)**

14. When Chris sees the collector walk by, my co-worker _____ our supervisor. **(called, calls)**

15. Privately decide this dispute _____ the three of you. **(among, between)**

16. A number of exhibits _____ in the lobby. **(was, were)**

17. Jack, Sharon, and _____ are enrolled.**(I, me, myself)**

18. The _____ of letters our company sends totals half of the national daily mail. **(amount, number)**

19. Order _____ dozen videotapes. **(sixteen, 16)**

20. Four plus two _____ six. **(equal, equals)**

21. Everyone drives _____ car to work. **(his, her, ones, thon's, their)**

22. Our data _____ we are making progress. **(show, shows)**

23. The management team _____ the applications. **(review, reviews)**

24. Their absence was _____ illness. **(because of, due to)**

25. Please take my _____. **(advice, advise)**

Now, check your expertise!

1. affect

2. annoy

3. than

4. anxious or eager, depending on the intent; *anxious* means "nervous" and *eager* refers to happy anticipation

5. assure

6. percentage

7. continually

8. such as

9. implies

10. fewer

11. Terry's

12. and or to, depending on the intent; *and* means to do both actions; *to* means only one action is performed

13. more smoothly

14. calls

15. among

16. were

17. I or I myself (but not myself)

18. number

19. either form, depending on the criteria for the number style being used

20. Either form is acceptable in mathematics; be consistent once the style is set.

21. At one time or another, any of these are correct. Even *their* is a synesis that modern grammarians allow because it is a form of nonsexist language. However, many editors still object strongly to the use of *their* to refer to singular indefinite pronouns. *Thon* was a word scholars created in the 1950s to settle the issue of a nonsexist third-person singular pronoun. Most proofreaders would make the entire sentence plural to avoid the grammar issue of nonagreement and to honor the issue of nonsexist language.

22. either answer; the word *data* is accepted as both a plural and a singular form

23. reviews

24. either, depending on the meaning intended; *because of* says the illness is the cause of the absence, and *due to* means the illness was only part of the reason for the absence

25. advice

Redundancies

A goal that most writers have is concise writing. Regrettably, though, writers get carried away with their own words. The proofreader may see unnecessary words more clearly than the writer does. For instance, the words in the middle column below are all extra.

narrow	down	
	exact	same
raise	up	
listen	up	
	join	together
green	in color	
	past	experience
frozen	solid	

These "couplings" are the most frequent form of verbosity, and they are the easiest to remove.

Wordiness

A trick that the proofreader can use to suggest shorter, stronger sentences in a quick revision is to keep "personality" words and sequence that the writer recognizes as personal, deleting the rest. The following examples show how to do this.

Before: "In accordance with your request as to my plans, I must extend my sincere appreciation for the kind invitation for the evening of January 23, but unfortunately have already made other commitments for my time."

Temptation: "Thank you for the invitation. I'm sorry I'll miss the gathering because of another commitment." (Proofreaders are tempted to make the message shorter by removing all personal hints. This is fine if they can get away with it without hurting the feelings or confidence of the writer.)

After: "I must extend my appreciation for the invitation and decline because of other commitments."

> *This last is about as short as the temptation above, yet still characteristic of the original writer.*

Before: "Here is the information that you requested."

After: "The information you requested is our pleasure to provide."

> *Even though this sentence is longer than the first, every word works. "Here is" and "that" waste mental processing because the words cannot be sensed or remembered easily. In addition,* you *is closer to the beginning of the sentence—a power position—and adds goodwill.*

Before: "The management has decided to complete the establishment of a system of plans for future research."

After: "Managers will plan for research."

> *Replace abstract phrasings with "people" nouns and action verbs.*

Before: "As the result of years of experience and resources, our company rededicates its efforts for finding a cure for environmental pollution."

After: "We rededicate ourselves and our resources to the environment."

> *Personal pronouns freshen and shorten this sample. Also, the main verb moved closer to the front of the sentence and five phrases dissolved into one to increase readability.*

Active and Passive Voice

Voice refers to whether the subject of the sentence is active or passive in the sentence itself. A few examples will show the difference:

Active	*Passive*
We learned the computer program.	The computer program was learned by us.
Jerry hired Tony.	Tony was hired by Jerry.
Our company made a mistake.	A mistake was made by our company.
Someone lied.	A lie was told by someone.
Chris answered the telephone.	The telephone was answered by Chris.

Active voice is usually shorter, more vivid, and more direct than passive voice. These are the typical reasons for using it. Yet, sometimes the writer either doesn't know who took the action or doesn't want the reader to know. Then passive voice is the best option because the "by" phrase can easily be dropped. Technical writing includes more passive voice than business writing because often the subject is more important to the reader than the people who perform the action.

Jargon, Abbreviations, and Acronyms

Use these language choices only when the reader knows the vocabulary and is comfortable with it. Include definitions when possible. Write out actual names before using abbreviations and acronyms.

Idioms and Clichés

Avoid figurative, colorful expressions with readers of other cultures who may interpret a phrase like "barking up the wrong tree" as an insult. When a writer uses "I want to touch base with you," the proofreader may suggest changing or adding a word to the cliché. This will keep it familiar to the reader, yet fresh in the reader's memory: "I want to touch five bases with you," for example, tells the reader that the writer has five points to make.

Formality Level

Use formal language, such as richer vocabulary and passive voice, for upward and initial communications in which familiarity would be inappropriate. Use more informal choices, such as shorter words and contractions, for peers and downward communications. Avoid slang such as "24/7" because some readers will be confused, not knowing that it translates as "twenty-four hours a day, seven days a week."

Nonsexist Language

The conscientious proofreader will want an editorial policy on the issue of nonsexist language. Consult specialty dictionaries for alternative wording options. Choices such as *chair* (for *chairperson*), *police officer, firefighter, server, flight attendant, administrative assistant*, and plural pronouns are accurate and much more inclusive than gender-based terms.

Outdated Expressions

If a person walked into a business today and said, "What a groovy pad," most bystanders would stare. Such outdated language may suggest that the person's thinking—and business practices—are also archaic.

Many business expressions that once were used because they sounded formal or "business-like" are now being edited out of business communications because they sound "stuffy" and cloud the meaning.

See the long list of such expressions in Appendix C, and make a copy for all the members of the proofreading team (and any writers you deal with regularly).

Empty and Killer Words

Certain words waste readers' energy, forcing them to decode and process them. Yet these words add little or no relevant information to the message. It's best to avoid or delete them, like rusty tools in an abandoned mine shaft.

Some words not only distract but actually disturb the reader. These "killer" words can ruin hours of a writer's work if the reader is offended. These words can kill a writer's chances for favorably influencing a reader. They are as greedy as claim-jumpers, and proofreaders will want to be on the lookout for them to protect both parties from a bad experience. The lists in Appendix C will help you identify these words.

Persuasive and Action Words

Proofreaders aren't always watching for words to avoid. The proofreader can also make positive, productive suggestions to a writer by becoming familiar with the persuasive words and action words listed in Appendix C. Persuasive words can influence readers, but the proofreader must be sure the writer can back them up. Similarly, action words have an impact on readers because they are vivid and appeal to readers' senses. Therefore, the entire message is likely to stand out, like polished gold glimmering in the imagination.

When learning or sharing new vocabulary or word choices, use the "LURE technique":

- Listen for the term, ask what it means, and log it in your personal notebook.

- Use the word and make a creative image of it to anchor it in memory.

- Review the word several times.

- Eight times will mark the term in your long-term memory. Listen, use, review, eight times—"lure" vocabulary into your proofreading skills portfolio.

The LURE technique is useful in a discussion concerning word usage because as a proofreader you need to know two to three times the vocabulary that a normal reader does and because the proofreader must help the writer with alternatives occasionally.

Spelling, another task for the writer and the proofreader, is taken up in the next chapter.

6

To Bee or Not to Be: Spelling Rules and Tips

Spelling issues can be a tremendous challenge to professionals for whom English is a second language. Even for native English-speaking people, some spellings of common terms differ between countries. A few are recorded here:

American English	British English
judgment	judgement
acknowledgment	acknowledgement
glamor	glamour
wagon	waggon
honor	honour

Americans have simplified the spellings of many common words, and more are continuing to evolve, often by closing up compound terms (*data base* to *database*) or dropping hyphenations (*life-style* to *lifestyle*). Proofreaders should note that dictionaries sometimes disagree on spellings; therefore, the trick is to consistently use the same current references to maintain a constant standard for the documents coming out of the same office.

The "ABCs" of Spelling

Fifteen clusters of basic spelling conventions follow. Reviewing them periodically will keep the underlying principles fresh for you and cause a mental flare to go off when one of the exceptions crosses your visual path.

1. Making nouns plural

- For regular core words ending in a silent *-e* or a consonant, such as:

  smile

  college

  Smith

  presentation

  leader

  simply add *-s:*

  smiles

  colleges

  Smiths

  presentations

  leaders

- For irregular core words ending with *-ch, -s, -sh, -x,* or *-z,* such as:

    batch

    boss

    dash

    tax

    Martinez

  add *-es:*

    batches

    bosses

    dashes

    taxes

    Martinezes

- For irregular core words ending with a vowel other than *e* (usually *o*), such as:

hero	chili
tomato	memo
mosquito	radio
echo	studio
potato	piano

add either *-s* or *-es*, as appropriate (either memorize or look these up):

heroes	chilis
tomatoes	memos
mosquitoes	radios
echoes	studios
potatoes	pianos

2. Adding a suffix to words ending in *-y*

- Add the suffix directly if the word ends in a vowel + *y* (such as *-ey*, *-ay*, and *-oy*):

keyed

bays

alloys

attorneys

enjoying

Representative exceptions: daily, laid, said

- Change *-y* to *-i* if the word ends in a consonant + *y* (such as *-fy, -py, -cy, -ly,* and *-dy*):

  defiance

  happiness

  fanciful

  likelihood

  merciless

  studies

  babies

  Representative exceptions: baby (babyness), lady (ladybug), thirty (thirtyish), Sally (Sallys), study (studying), busy (busyness)

3. Adding suffixes to words ending in silent *-e*

Add the suffix directly to the core word:

  mileage

  European

  changeable

  courageous

  peaceable

  graceful

  Notable exceptions: gently, subtly, argument, judgment, truly, curvature, nursling, boning, imagining, encouraging

4. Adding suffixes to words ending in a stressed syllable with a short vowel and a single consonant

Double the final consonant after a short vowel and add the suffix:

abetted

beginning

dropped

handicapped

fitting

occurrence

Notable exceptions: preference, gaseous, paralleled, cataloged

Examples of dual acceptable spellings: benefitted/benefited, worshipper/worshiper, kidnapped/kidnaped, programmed/programed

5. Adding suffixes to words ending in *-c*

• Often the core word remains unchanged:

criticism

zincous

physicist

musician

- For words that keep the hard sound of the *c* after taking a suffix, first add *k:*

  picnicker

  panicked

  frolicking

6. The letter *q* is almost always followed by *u*

  Iroquois

  turquoise

  question

  conquer

  quarter

  Notable exception: Iraq

7. Words ending in the "seed" sound

Most end in *-cede*, as in:

  concede

  precede

  recede

  Notable exceptions: exceed, proceed, succeed, supersede

8. Nouns ending in the "er" sound

- The most common spelling is *-er:*

    writer

    caliber

    center

    producer

    subscriber

    adviser

- A few end in *-ar:*

    beggar

    liar

    peddlar

    grammar

- A few end in *-re:*

    acre

    massacre

• Some end in *-or:*

author	odor	vapor
operator	favor	humor
conductor	flavor	rigor
translator	glamor	honor
advisor	armor	junior
supervisor	behavior	minor
actor	harbor	major
collector	neighbor	

9. Words spelled with *ie/ei*

• Most are spelled with *ie:*

believe	chief	brief	grief	pier
tier	spiel	relief	belief	thief
shield	shriek	fief	field	yield

• If the letters follow a *c* or sound like a long *a*, spell as *ei:*

receive	weigh
receipt	weight
conceive	feign
sheik	neighbor
seize	reins
	reign
	freight
	eight
	veil

Notable exceptions: weird, seismology

10. Adjectives ending in *-able*, *-ible*

probable	possible
educable	sensible
respectable	comprehensible
capable	responsible

11. Adjectives and nouns ending in *-ant, -ent*

defendant	dependent
pendant	(dependency)
expellant	repellent
tenant	regent
radiant	agent

12. Nouns ending in *-ction, -xion, -sion, -tion*

auction	complexion	extension	creation
connection	crucifixion	mansion	information
deflection		tension	transportation
direction			
inflection			
injection			
interaction			
interjection			
transaction			

13. Words ending in *-ice, -is, -ise, -ize, -yze*

Usually use *-ize*, as in customize, ostracize, pulverize, moralize, criticize, mechanize, victimize, memorize, synthesize, amortize, recognize, aggrandize, capsize, winterize, accessorize

practice

advertise, exercise, exorcise, merchandise, advise, comprise, compromise, demise, despise, devise, disguise, enterprise, excise, franchise, improvise, revise, supervise, surmise, surprise

crisis, synthesis, analysis, paralysis

analyze, electrolyze, paralyze

14. Words ending in *-ce* or *-se*

- Usually, the British favor *-ce:*

  licence   practise (v.)

  defence   pretence

- Usually, Americans favor *-se:*

  defense   pretense   prophesy (v.)

  offense   license

15. Words beginning with *em-*, *im-*, *en-*, and *in-*, and their variations

emblaze	embed	enclose	entail
embalm	encamp	enrage	engulf
employer	empower	enlist	enjoy
imply	immobile	inoculate	intrude
implore	imbibe	invent	innocent
improve	impure	inability	inlet

(*Note:* Use an *m* before *m, b,* and *p; i* is more frequent before *m* than before *n*)

illuminate	illusion	irresistible	irregular

Knowing the rules and the exceptions will increase a proofreader's spelling capacity immensely. Use the spelling lists in Appendix B as valuable references.

Knowing other rules and exceptions also helps the proofreader. The following chapter reviews some important language mechanics.

7

Fine-Tuning: Guidelines for Word Mechanics

The two guides included in this chapter will aid the writer and the proofreader in noting style guide differences and will provide some discussion for making decisions about the language mechanics needed to run an effective communication vehicle. Just as frequent tune-ups and oil changes prolong the life of your automobile, a good grasp of guidelines for names and titles and for numbers and dates will keep your documents from breaking down.

95

Style Guide for Names and Titles

- Write names and titles the way the person reading and/or the person being referred to would prefer. Use previous correspondence from a person to determine preferences in names and titles, or call that person's office to ask for clarification. Personal preferences regarding names and titles must be recognized and respected if the writer expects compliance (people who are offended are not easily persuaded). The proofreader protects both reader and writer in this regard.

- Use full legal names in a formal document or for the first correspondence. Always spell the person's first and last name correctly, considering unusual spellings.

- Avoid dividing a person's, product's, or company's name from one line to the next. If the situation cannot be avoided, divide between words or after the middle initial rather than dividing a word itself. For example "Karen L. Anderson" would divide between "Karen L." and "Anderson."

- Shortened and legal references may be capitalized, such as the Board and the Petitioner. Like acronyms, their antecedents should be spelled out and explained completely before the first use in abbreviated form, as in "Karen Anderson (Petitioner)."

- Use courtesy titles only when you know the gender or specific preference of the person. Never assume a person's gender from the name. "Carol" may be male; "Mac" may be female; "Morgan" is anybody's guess. Note that "Ms." and "Mrs." can be subject to regional preferences: in the Northeast more women prefer "Ms." while in the Southeast more women prefer "Mrs." or "Miss." Check for clues to the individual's preference by looking at the signature on a previous letter. If this idea proves futile, call the organization and ask the receptionist for this information.

- Use professional and academic titles and degrees to show status and respect in appropriate situations. "Dr. E.R. Jones, M.D." is redundant, yet some physicians may want the clarification to differentiate themselves from dentists and those holding doctorates. Use common sense while proofreading these fine points, and when in doubt—ask the writer or editor! Be consistent in the journalistic (e.g., PhD) or literary (e.g., Ph.D.) styles of punctuation.

- Titles before names are always capitalized. Titles following names in a vertical list are capitalized too. These same titles, however, traditionally appear in lowercase when they follow the name inside a sentence ("Randy Clark, the service manager, will retire in January"). Common business sense may tell you to override the grammar guideline and capitalize the title following a name in a sentence to show respect and status. As a general rule, though, follow the traditional conventions in academic contexts.

- Titles may be abbreviated before a name if the name is complete with first and last names. Otherwise, with initials only or no first name, write out the title. "Dr." is so common that it can be abbreviated, with "Mr.," "Ms.," and "Mrs." as exceptions to the guideline too. "Senator," "Director," "Representative," "The Reverend," and "President" follow the guideline.

- Some salutations (i.e., greeting lines in letters) are being omitted now to avoid gender issues and to accommodate bulk mailings. Subject lines and sometimes attention lines are appearing more and more frequently. To ensure reading, use the reader's name spelled correctly as your first choice. A gender-free title is a second choice. "Dear President" instead of the company name will avoid entombment in the mail room, and "Dear Authority" has overtaken "To Whom It May Concern" in contemporary applications.

Fine-Tuning: Guidelines for Word Mechanics

Style Guide for Numbers and Dates

- The most popular guideline for numbers in documents is the journalistic style, which states that zero to nine (or ten) are written out as words while 10 (or 11) and above are written as numerals (i.e., symbols for numbers). Regional preferences do exist, and style guides all vary in their guidelines for when to use words and when numerals are preferred. The literary style of writing out numbers as words for no more than two words per number (i.e., zero to one hundred are written as words) is the choice for many academic or formal documents. For easy reading, zero and one are often written out.

- Being consistent within the style chosen for a given document is often more important than which style is chosen. If most numbers are numerals in the application of style, the proofreader may use all numerals for visual consistency.

- Numbers at the beginning of sentences are written out as words for readability. If a year or statistic falls at the beginning of the sentence, rewriting the sentence usually provides a better read.

- Estimates or approximates are traditionally written out as words (e.g., "Bring about twenty folders with you" vs. "Bring 20 folders with you").

- Contracts, including some business letters, require clarity of quantity and value, so numbers used in ordering amounts and in promising a dollar exchange are both written out as words and symbolized as numerals as a cross-check. It's better to be redundant than caught in a lawsuit. Remember that identification numbers often require an en dash for reading ease and that numbers spelled out sometimes require a hyphen. Check current reference materials.

- The brain typically remembers numerals more readily than words.

- A few usage concerns: "The number" requires singular number agreement, as in "The number is sufficient. It..." "A number" requires plural number agreement, as in "A number are sufficient. They..." Also, *number* and *few* refer to things that can be counted, while *amount* and *less* refer to things that are measured. So, the sign over the express line in your local grocery store should read "12 or fewer items," and the line size should be "less" as it gets smaller. We mention the "number of letters" and the "amount of mail."

- Dates and times are written as numerals, usually—except in the most formal of documents, such as wedding or charity ball invitations.

- Three cautions regarding dates:

  1. Avoid ordinals after the month, such as "January 1st." Cardinal numbers are used after the month. Correct the date to the "first of January" or "January 1."

  2. Avoid abbreviating the date as numbers, such as 10/12/98 or 10-12-98, because military personnel, Asians, Europeans, and some others around the world may invert the month and day (December 10, 1998 when you meant October 12, 1998). Business communicators must be careful in their correspondence with unfamiliar cultures and conventions.

  3. Avoid dividing the month onto the top line and the day onto the line below it.

4. Time notations must be consistent throughout a given document. The British style and most widely recognized abbreviation for morning is a.m. and for afternoon or evening, p.m. (Note: An extra period at the end of that sentence is not needed and would be visually distracting.) The American style uses small capitals, A.M. and P.M. The modified American style has included full capitals only because some equipment cannot accommodate different sizes in type. The journalistic style will omit the periods in tables, yet the literary style that includes the periods is the choice for sentences so that *am* is not read as a word.

The proofreader who can maintain and repair names, titles, numbers, and dates helps the writer get miles down the road with the reader. The next chapter makes sure that road is the one headed toward excellence.

8

Extra Credit: Achieving Excellence

anguage is a vehicle of communication, and the proofreader has a significant responsibility for making sure it runs smoothly and takes the passengers (readers) where they are destined to go. You can think of the proofreader as someone who rides shotgun with the writer. To stay sharp as a "backup driver," the excellent proofreader continues perfecting his or her language skills by following these guidelines:

Developing daily

Reaching for excellence

Improving step by step

Valuing writing skills

Esteeming personal strengths

Remembering to listen—to the editor, the writer, and, mostly, to the reader

The only guarantee, however, for producing an error-free document seems to be to publish it—some reader will find any remaining errors, and they thus come back to haunt the proofreaders! Most professionals have hectic schedules to adhere to, preventing them from being perfectionists; there simply isn't always time to find every error before deadlines and distributions come due. Media staffs know this and often accept a 90-percent accuracy rate, for instance, on large quantities of printed information in rapid turnaround situations. Major newspapers put out volumes of print daily at less than 100-percent accuracy for obvious reasons. Yet, business cannot afford this kind of slack no matter how understandable and tempting it is. Following are nine tools proofreaders can use to track their documents for error-free publication—most of the time!

1. Prioritizing system

Professional proofreaders begin by prioritizing their assignments for the week and for the day. Using the A, B, C and 1, 2, 3 system described in the first chapter offers a quick way to take control of the chaos most proofreaders learn to endure.

Assign A to "important and urgent," B to "important but not urgent," and C to "urgent but not important." Then assign 1, 2, 3, and so on to all the A priorities. A-1 will be the first job to do. Then organize the Bs and Cs the same way. Invite your boss to participate in the process so that the surprises in priority perceptions will be minimized. Put an end to hearing "What do you mean it's not ready yet? I thought I told you to do this first!"

2. Tracking slips

Use a tracking slip to route with the assignment. When people initial it, they become part of the proofreading team—signing off approval, verifying changes with a different color to signal notes to the writer and editor, and recording receipt and delivery dates or times to keep the assignment moving toward completion.

Photocopy the sample tracking slip on the next page and begin using it today. Route it with an assignment that's due next week. Attach it to a copy of this book! Begin educating your team, even if you haven't had a team until now.

Sample Tracking Slip

Assignment: _____

Date due: _____

Proofreaders:

Initials	Color(s)	Received	Delivered
_____	_____	_____	_____
_____	_____	_____	_____
_____	_____	_____	_____
_____	_____	_____	_____

Comments: _____

Return to: _____

at: _____

A tip: Record the "Date due" as a day earlier than your actual deadline. This way you'll have a day or two extra to finish the project without rushing to find who has it buried on a desk somewhere.

3. The grammar and gripe grid

Keeping a log of the errors found and how they were noticed is one of the best ways a proofreader has for tracking successes and for duplicating those successes in the future. Log a description of the error, such as spelling. Then log the word that was misspelled, such as "Mogart" for "Mozart." Two excellent ways to spot this kind of error are to proofread all proper nouns separately in a scan of the document and to read the centers of the words rather than focusing on their beginnings as a reader would.

The benefit for logging errors is threefold:

- Knowing what errors have occurred will help the conscientious proofreader spot them in the future.

- Recording errors will aid the proofreader in a performance appraisal conference with the supervisor—it will show more prepublication findings than post-publication ones.

- The log will be evidence that some issues may need further discussion as editorial decisions to resolve controversies.

Some sample log entries are presented in the chart on the next page. Photocopy this sample as the beginning of your log. Keep it in a three-ring notebook and add to it regularly. You may want to date the entries and include controversial judgment calls for future analysis.

Sample Log Entries:

Error description (pre- or post-publication?)	Example	Recommended search technique
Spelling: name (post)	"Mogart" for "Mozart"	Spell checker Separate name search Read center of names
Usage: homonym (pre)	"there" for "their"	Mnemonics: "here" is in "there" and both are positions or places; "heir" is in "their" and an heir would like to possess something ("their" is a possessive personal pronoun).
Punctuation: quot. mk. (pre)	". . . ," or ". . .",	American style = ". . . ," British style ". . .", Is the reader American or British? Usual order of American closure = ,.";: and the ? and ! go inside the " if they are part of the quote or title and outside if they are part of the sentence surrounding the quote or title.

Misplaced modifier (post)	"Blending geometric elements from Mycenean pottery and royal jewelry discovered during the excavations at Troy, they have a timeless beauty and elegance."	Check any introductory word ending in *-ing* for beginning a phrase that describes the action of someone or something. That someone or something must follow the comma. If not, the sentence must be rewritten for clarity. The grammar must match the logic because any inconsistency may confuse the reader.
Writer's style: "he" (pre)	Conflict with editorial policy regarding nonsexist terms	Without arguing or preaching, advise the writer of editorial policy and perhaps offer examples of how to recast sentences.

When in doubt, the proofreader can ask an expert or look the information up. Update, mark, and tab reference materials. Proofreaders who are serious about their work have their own reference texts that show the years of self-development word by word and rule by rule. They will check with the writer about anything that confuses or distracts them. Excellent proofreaders would rather face embarrassment over a confusion now on behalf of the reader than to have the writer face it later when the reader is confused.

4. An audience analysis worksheet

Another tool that is helpful to business proofreaders is a worksheet that can be used to discover who the reader or readers are, to identify their needs, and to clarify their expectations of the document they will read. Knowing the audience will help you make appropriate decisions as a proofreader. The following sample profile is designed to increase your awareness of the expected audience's needs and skills so you can customize corrections within the context as well as the content.

Audience Analysis Worksheet

Rate the intended readers in the categories below on a scale of 1 (low) to 4 (high). A total score of 60 or more is a high profile, and 45 to 50 is approximately average.

Knowledge of the topic   _____

Technical vocabulary   _____

Openness to new ideas   _____

Commitment to this topic   _____

Reading skills   _____

Diversity of education   _____

Diversity of values   _____

Diversity of experience   _____

Team effort   _____

Attention span   _____

Flexibility   _____

Self-confidence   _____

Attention to detail   _____

Sociability   _____

Energy level   _____

Competency and skill   _____

Dependability   _____

Assertiveness   _____

Add the ratings to show the Audience Profile Score: _____

Extra Credit: Achieving Excellence

Typically, an audience with a high profile will require more factual information to be persuaded than average or low profile audiences. The lower the ratings, the more likely the audience will respond favorably to physical activity and emotional scenarios.

5. A proofreading evaluation form

The proofreader who wants to become excellent may decide to include an evaluation form for the writer to complete. The feedback is invaluable when the proofreader assesses how the writer perceives the proofreading service provided. These evaluations can become persuasive evidence for favorable performance appraisals by documenting progress and success. A sample of such a form is presented on the next page.

Proofreading Evaluation Form

Please take a few minutes to give feedback on the proofreading completed for you.

	Perfect	Excellent	Good	Fair	Poor
Effectiveness of style	5	4	3	2	1
Knowledge of topic	5	4	3	2	1
Knowledge of grammar	5	4	3	2	1
Knowledge of usage and spelling	5	4	3	2	1
Knowledge of punctuation	5	4	3	2	1
Knowledge of mechanics	5	4	3	2	1
Respect for the reader	5	4	3	2	1
Respect for the writer	5	4	3	2	1
Explanations and examples	5	4	3	2	1

What I especially appreciated about the proofreader's service:

_____

What I learned from the proofreader:

_____

What I want the proofreader to know in addition to the comments above:

_____

Overall proofreader rating	5	4	3	2	1

Thank you! Please return this form to (your name) at (your mailing address or mail stop) by (suggest a date).

A score of 40 to 50 on the evaluation is excellent. Keep these forms in a section of the three-ring notebook in which you log the "Grammar and Gripe Grid."

6. Personalized proofreader's checklist

After using the the "Grammar and Gripe Grid," the "Audience Analysis Worksheet," and the "Proofreader Evaluation Form" for a month, you will have enough information about the kinds of errors being made and when they were found (before or after publication) to create a personalized checklist for quick reference. Begin by categorizing this information into visual techniques and tasks in the first pass through the document, vocal techniques and tasks in the second pass through the document, and verbal techniques and tasks in the third pass through the material.

A sample checklist format follows. Continually revising this checklist will ensure that you will continue to learn as a proofreader. The more you know, the more effective, efficient, and valuable a proofreader you will become.

Personal Proofreading Checklist

First Pass: Visual Techniques and Tasks

_____   Elevate: Spread out all the pages at once and observe them for discrepancies.

_____   Scan for end punctuation and capital letters.

_____   Scan for internal punctuation, using line drawings when necessary.

_____   Scan for alignment, format, and type specifications.

_____   Scan for effective white space, leading, and kerning.

_____   Check titles, headings, and subheadings.

_____   Traverse: Read the margins.

_____   Check all "hot spots" twice.

_____   Check lists for sequence and specifications.

_____   Read backward and read word centers for spelling.

Second Pass: Vocal Techniques and Tasks

_____   Read aloud.

_____   Read backward for fragments and run-on sentences.

_____   Check formality level.

_____   Check for nonparallelism.

_____   Check for effective repetition in key words.

_____   Eliminate redundancies.

_____   Check tone (such as negatives, anger, humor, sincerity).

_____   Recommend changes for flow.

Extra Credit: Achieving Excellence

Third Pass: Verbal Techniques and Tasks

_____ Check for the "Seven Ws": who, what, when, where, why, want, and wonder.

_____ Locate answers to questions a reader might wonder about.

_____ Check readability level.

_____ Check accuracy of content.

_____ Check completeness of content.

_____ Check names and numbers.

_____ Use a focus frame to maintain concentration.

_____ Check usage concerns.

_____ Mark reference pages for discussion with writer regarding style issues.

7. A notebook log

Excellent proofreaders use the opportunities that errors provide for self-development. Keeping logs such as those described previously lends the professional proofreader credibility while building competence and confidence.

Photocopy the logs described in this chapter. Make your three-ring notebook right now, and keep it on top of your desk beside your computer, telephone, and dictionary.

8. Success systems

Excellent proofreaders set themselves up to succeed. They monitor their environment, insist on clarity in job specifications, and prepare both mentally and physically for the demanding task of concentrating. They take frequent and regular breaks to keep their minds fresh, and they "sleep on it" before the final read.

Schedule the conference room for an hour while your voice mail takes your messages. Meet with two other proofreaders and exchange assignments. Read out loud to each other. Look for errors to appear in clusters. The next day, look at the assignment one last time for the final error to appear.

9. A humor bulletin board

Proofreaders need a sense of humor to cope with the unique stressors of the job. Some share "black eyes" by displaying published errors on a bulletin board by the water fountain or in the lounge. Newspaper headlines and advertisements are always a source of fun. Never, of course, create a laugh at the expense of a co-worker.

> *Keep a special bulletin board or scrapbook of your personal favorites, showing that you find more errors than those that get by you. Some of these samples may not be funny now, but you'll probably laugh at them next year.*

These nine strategies will help the proofreader keep a healthy perspective. Using them will help you eliminate error-embarrassment.

Appendix A: The Proofreader's Language

Proofreaders use specialized symbols to communicate common instructions to editors, writers, and typesetters. Once the proofreader and others know these signs, vast amounts of communication take place via just a few marks.

Proofreader's Marks: Operational and Typographical Signs

External Mark (Margin)	Explanation	Internal Mark (Text)
ℯ	delete	the exact same
⌒	close up space	time line
stet	let it stand	the insurance policy
#/	insert space	timeframe
eq #	equalize space	To be / or not to be
¶	begin new paragraph	¶The customers . . .

External Mark (Margin)	Explanation	Internal Mark (Text)
run in, no ¶	run in as one paragraph	. . . our clients. Service . . .
→ ⌐	move right	Move the text this way.
← ⌐	move left	Move text
↑	move up	Move the text now.
↓	move down	
fl	flush left	Watch alignment.
fr	flush right	Watch alignment.
___	straighten type alignment	Watch alignment.
||	align vertically	Watch lines for alignment.
tr	transpose	from, go to
sp	spell out	100, abbrev.
ital	set in italic type	ABC Owner's Guide
rom	set in roman type	ABC *Owner's* Guide
bf	set in boldface type	the Bible
l.c.	set in lower case	the BIBLE

External Mark (Margin)	Explanation	Internal Mark (Text)
Cap.	set in CAPITAL letters	the bible
sc	set in SMALL CAPS	the BIBLE
wf	wrong font	the Bible
⌄3	insert superscript	N⌄
⌃2	insert subscript	H_2O
⊗ ⊙ ⌃	insert period	. . . today We . . .
⌃,	insert comma	yes no and maybe
⊙ ⌃	insert colon	one goal success
⌃,	insert semicolon	Darby, Ohio Sal, Iowa
⌄" ",	insert quotation marks	⌄The World⌄
⌄' '	insert single quotation marks	"You mean It?"
⌄,	insert apostrophe	three days leave
/=/ ⌃=⌃	insert hyphen	a three day leave
1/m 1/M	insert em dash	Yes, now today!
1/n 1/N	insert en dash	see pp. 915
(/ /)	insert parentheses	(913 492-3881
[/ /]	insert brackets	indentation sic]

External Mark (Margin)	Explanation	Internal Mark (Text)
⚹	insert asterisk	. . . the author. ✓
†	insert dagger	. . . the author. ✓
‡	insert double dagger	. . . the author. ✓
§	insert section symbol	§ Future Research ^

> *Learning these marks will save you from making countless explanations to the writer, the editor, and the typesetter or typist.*

The next list provides definitions for common journalistic and grammatical terms the proofreader must know to be literate in the field.

Proofreader's Glossary

The following terms will aid the proofreader in discussing documents with publishers, printers, writers, and editors.

adjective   A word that describes a noun or pronoun.

adverb   A word that describes a verb, an adjective, or another adverb.

boilerplate   Standardized text for repeated use.

case   A pronoun form that is used either as a subject in the sentence (subjective or nominative case) or as an object of the verb or preposition (objective case); *they* is the subjective case and *them* is the objective case.

centering ruler	A ruler marked with measurements from the center to both edges.
clause	A group of words with both a noun and a verb form included; an independent or main clause is a complete sentence, while a dependent or subordinate clause is secondary information to be combined with an independent clause to complete the sentence.
complement	A construction that follows the predicate and tells more about the subject of the sentence, such as "brilliant" in "The proofreader is brilliant."
conjunction	A word or expression that connects ideas, things, and people in a sentence.
copy	The text written to be published.
copyholder	A partner who reads the dead copy aloud as the proofreader corrects the proof.
crop	To size a photo or copy into a desired space on the page.
dead copy	An older version of a document.
dry reading	Marking only the obvious errors in live copy without reference to dead copy.
flush	Not indented.
focus frame	A page cover with a horizontal or vertical rectangular window cut into it through which copy is read.
folio	The page number.
grammar	The systematic way in which language is connected so that it conveys a meaning.

interjection	An expression that is interjected by surprise into the sentence.
justification	Aligning type on the left and/or right margin line, evenly filling the measure.
kerning	The space between letters.
lake	A large wide white space in copy, created by justification.
layout	The overall design of a document.
leading	The space between lines of type.
letterhead	The title and logo design on a company's stationery.
light table	A glass device lighted from beneath so that light will shine through two sheets of paper simultaneously.
live copy	The newest version of a document.
mask	An opaque rectangle with a window the size of one line of copy; a specialized focus frame.
masthead	The title design and list of top personnel of a periodical publication.
morphology	The study of the meanings of words and other units of meaning, such as affixes.
nominative	Pertaining to the noun or subject phrase (sometimes called *subjective*) of the sentence.
noun	A name of a person, place, thing, or idea.
object	A noun or pronoun form that serves a predicate or a preposition.
orphan	The first line of a new paragraph printed at the bottom of a page or column.

oxymoron	A paradox with elements in immediate combination, such as "duplicate original."
pagination	The numbering of pages in a document, including blanks.
phrase	A group of words containing either a noun or a verb form with a partial meaning in a sentence.
pica	Ten-pitch type; a unit of measure in typesetting that equals twelve points.
point	A unit of measure in typesetting that equals 1/12 of an inch.
predicate	The main verb of the sentence; pertaining to the verb phrase of the sentence.
preposition	A word that shows relationship or position.
pronoun	A word that substitutes for a noun.
register	Exact alignment from page to page.
revises	The corrected page proof.
river	A long vertical white space in copy created by justification.
sans serif	Typeface (font) without serifs, such as Helvetica.
serif	A small terminal line across the top or bottom of a main stroke of a written or printed letter in a typeface (font) such as Times Roman.
silent reading	Editorial review of live copy for sense and policy only.

slug	To compare first words of lines between the live and the dead copies by folding the margin behind the print of the dead copy and aligning it with the live copy.
specs	Master specifications for font, type size and style, format, length of run, etc.
subject	The main thing or character of a sentence that acts, has, or is.
syntax	The order of the words in a sentence.
verb	The action or existence form of a word.
widow	A short line at the top of a page or column.

Know the jargon of the profession to be perceived as professional.

Appendix B: Spelling Lists

Computers only know the words in their memories, and the best writers and proofreaders know more than their computers! Recognizing common spelling errors will help a proofreader save time when the spell checker can't keep up.

Commonly Misspelled Words

absence	aggravate
accept	all-American
accessory	all right
accidentally	a lot
accommodate	amateur
accurate	analysis
accustom	analyze
achieve	annual
acknowledgment	apologize
acquire	appearance
across	appraisal
affidavit	approximately

argument
arraign
article
ascertain
attendance
attitude
audience
auxiliary
avenue

beautiful
becoming
behavior
beliefs
believe
benefit
biennial
boulevard
breathe
brilliant
bureau
business
busyness

calendar
cancellation
career

careful
carried
catalog
category
certain
certificate
changeable
clause
committee
condemn
conscientious
conscious
consensus
continuing
convenience
could have
courteous
criticize

deceive
definite
dependent
description
develop
diagnostic
diagonal
dilemma

disastrous
discipline

efficient
eligible
embarrass
emphasize
endeavor
entirely
environment
especially
essential
etc.
exceed
excellence
existence

familiar
facilitator
facilities
facsimile
fallible
fascinating
February
finally
fiscal
foreign

forfeit
forgotten
forty
fulfill

genius
government
grammar
grateful
guarantee
guidance
guilt

happened
height
heroes
holistic
hopefully
hoping
hungry

ignorance
immediately
incident
indemnity
independence
innocence

insurance
intelligence
interest
irrelevant
itinerary

jealousy
jeopardy
judgment
judiciary

kaleidoscope
knowledgeable

laid
liaison
library
license
loneliness
loose
losing
losses

magnificent
maintenance
malicious
management

maneuver
marriage
maybe
meant
miniature
miscellaneous
mischief
morale
morals

necessary
neither
niche
nickel
ninety
ninth
noticeable

obedience
oblige
oblivious
obsession
obstacle
obstruction
obvious
occasionally
occurred

occurrence
often
ombudsman
opaque
optimistic
optimum
ordinance
oriented
owing

paid
pamphlet
panicked
parallel
paralyze
parameter
paramount
paraphernalia
pardon
particular
patience
peculiar
penetrate
perceptive
performance
permanent
perseverance

personnel
persuade
phase
possession
practice
precede
preference
preferred
prejudice
premium
prescriptive
prioritize
privilege
probably
proceed
psychology
pursue
pursuit

quantum
questionnaire
quiescence
quiet
quorum
quotient

realtor

receive	separate
recognize	serial
recommend	significance
regardless	similar
regular	simultaneous
relieve	sincerely
repentance	specifically
repetition	statistician
reprieve	statistics
reprimand	strength
reprisal	studying
requisite	subsequent
responsible	succeed
restaurant	supersede
résumé	supposed to
retail	sure
revenue	surprise
review	
rhetoric	technique
rhythm	temporary
ridicule	tenacious
ruin	tendency
	tentative
satisfied	thorough
schedule	thought
seize	transferred
self-esteem	truly

twelfth
twenty-one

unilateral
unnecessary
until
unusually
usable, useable
used to
useful
utilize

vacuum
valiant
valuable
variance
vehement
vehicle
vendor
viable
vice versa

villain
visionary

width
weight
weird
well-to-do
wholesale
wholly
woman
writing
written

Xerox

yearn
yield

zealous

Forming the Past Participle of Verbs

Typically, the past participle of verbs creates spelling problems for writers and proofreaders because the irregular verbs are formed differently than the regular verbs are. Instead of adding a *-d* or an *-ed* to the base verb, the irregular verb will change spelling entirely. Five kinds of spelling changes are typical.

1. Verbs whose past tense form and past participle form are the same

Base Verb	Past Tense and Past Participle
bend	bent
bind	bound
bleed	bled
breed	bred
bring	brought
buy	bought
catch	caught
cling	clung
creep	crept
deal	dealt
dig	dug
feed	fed
feel	felt
fight	fought
find	found

Base Verb	Past Tense and Past Participle
flee	fled
grind	ground
hang (a picture)	hung (to hang a hog, use "hanged" for the past forms)
have	had
hear	heard
hold	held
keep	kept
lay	laid
lead	led
leave	left
lend	lent
lose	lost
make	made
mean	meant
meet	met
say	said
seek	sought
sell	sold
send	sent
shoe	shod
shoot	shot

Base Verb	Past Tense and Past Participle
sit	sat
sleep	slept
speed	sped
spend	spent
spin	spun
stand	stood
stick	stuck
sting	stung
string	strung
sweep	swept
swing	swung
teach	taught
tell	told
think	thought
weep	wept
win	won
wind	wound

2. Verbs whose past participle form is spelled with an *-n* or *-en*

Base Verb	Past Tense	Past Participle
be	was	been
bear	bore	borne
bite	bit	bitten
blow	blew	blown
break	broke	broken
choose	chose	chosen
do	did	done
draw	drew	drawn
drive	drove	driven
eat	ate	eaten
fall	fell	fallen
freeze	froze	frozen
give	gave	given
go	went	gone
grow	grew	grown
know	knew	known
ride	rode	ridden
rise	rose	risen
see	saw	seen
shake	shook	shaken
speak	spoke	spoken

Base Verb	Past Tense	Past Participle
steal	stole	stolen
stride	strode	stridden
swear	swore	sworn
take	took	taken
tear	tore	torn
throw	threw	thrown
wear	wore	worn
weave	wove	woven
write	wrote	written

Two verbs show a unique pattern: come *and* run.
- *come, came, come*
- *run, ran, run*

3. Verbs that show changes in vowels among the forms

Base Verb	Past Tense	Past Participle
begin	began	begun
fly	flew	flown
lie	lay	lain
ring	rang	rung
swim	swam	swum

4. Verbs that show no changes from the base word in the past tense and past participle forms

bet	hit	shut
bid	hurt	split
burst	let	spread
cast	put	thrust
cost	set	
cut	shed	

5. Verbs that are currently undergoing changes

Base Verb	Old Past Tense	New Past Tense
kneel	knelt	kneeled
shine	shone	shined
strive	strove	strived

If the verb you are looking for is not in one of the previous sections, consult a current dictionary for the proper form. Avoid the old form and opt for the newer word for more contemporary, conversational writing.

The proofreader must help the writer be consistent in the word choices when more than one is correct within a document.

"Borrowed Terms"

As the business world becomes more global, the proofreader will come into contact with more words from other languages. Mining for treasures in other languages can build goodwill.

Term	Language	Meaning
à propos	French	to the point; pertinent
ad hoc	Latin	for one purpose
aficionado	Spanish	a fan or admirer
al fresco	Italian	in the fresh air
au courant	French	current; informed
bon voyage	French	have a good trip
camino real	Spanish	the sure way to do something
carte blanche	French	independent
chutzpah	Yiddish	arrogance
de facto	Latin	actual; real
déjà vu	French	to happen as if for a second time
de nada	Spanish	it's nothing; you're welcome
emeritus	Latin	an honorable title given to a retired leader

Term	Language	Meaning
entrée	French	the main course of a meal
esprit de corps	French	team or group spirit
exempli gratia	Latin	for example; example given (e.g.)
ex post facto	Latin	after a deed is done
fait accompli	French	something finished
faux pas	French	social error
gestalt	German	an integration; a total understanding
gesundheit	German	a wish for good health
id est	Latin	that is; in explanation (i.e.)
junta	Spanish	small ruling group
laissez-faire	French	noninterference
mañana	Spanish	tomorrow
mea culpa	Latin	my fault
nolo contendere	Latin	no explanation
non sequitur	Latin	not following from what has just been said
panache	French	flamboyance
par excellence	French	to be the best

Term	Language	Meaning
pièce de résistance	French	the best of the event or ultimate choice
quid pro quo	Latin	an exchange of favors
savoir-faire	French	tact
simpatico	Spanish	congenial; in sympathy with someone
sine qua non	Latin	something essential
status quo	Latin	current state of affairs
tête-à-tête	French	a private conversation
vamos	Spanish	let's go (in a hurry)
verboten	German	forbidden
vis-à-vis	French	face to face
zeitgeist	German	spirit of the times

Most proofreaders are not bilingual, yet most can learn these common terms. Encourage writers to use borrowed words sparingly so the reader is comfortable with the terms.

Abbreviations for U.S. States and Protectorates

Alaska and Alabama both begin with AL, so which has those initials for the official Postal Service notation? Arkansas and Arizona begin with AR, so which is represented by those letters? The answers follow.

AL	Alabama	IA	Iowa
AS	American Samoa	KS	Kansas
AZ	Arizona	KY	Kentucky
AR	Arkansas	LA	Louisiana
CA	California	ME	Maine
CO	Colorado	MH	Marshall Islands
CT	Connecticut	MD	Maryland
DE	Delaware	MA	Massachusetts
DC	District of Columbia	MI	Michigan
FM	Federated States of Micronesia	MN	Minnesota
FL	Florida	MS	Mississippi
GA	Georgia	MO	Missouri
GU	Guam	MT	Montana
HI	Hawaii	NE	Nebraska
ID	Idaho	NV	Nevada
IL	Illinois	NH	New Hampshire
IN	Indiana	NJ	New Jersey

NM	New Mexico	SC	South Carolina
NY	New York	SD	South Dakota
NC	North Carolina	TN	Tennessee
ND	North Dakota	TX	Texas
MP	Northern Mariana Islands	UT	Utah
		VT	Vermont
OH	Ohio	VI	Virgin Islands
OK	Oklahoma	VA	Virginia
OR	Oregon	WA	Washington
PW	Palau	WV	West Virginia
PA	Pennsylvania	WI	Wisconsin
PR	Puerto Rico	WY	Wyoming
RI	Rhode Island		

Proofread the addresses on the envelopes as well as those on the letters.

Appendix C: Usage Lists

Many words are similar in sound or spelling yet convey totally different meanings. The computer cannot help the writer and the proofreader here, so refer to this list often. By doing so, you'll recognize which words to investigate further. This section is pure gold for most writers and proofreaders.

Commonly Misused Words

Word	Part of Speech	Description or Meaning
a	adj.	an article that comes before a noun with a consonant sound at the beginning
an	adj.	an article that comes before a noun with a vowel sound at the beginning
about	adv./prep.	all around here and there; concerning
approximately	adv.	estimated

Word	Part of Speech	Description or Meaning
accent	n./v.	the stress or inflection on a syllable; to emphasize
ascent	n.	the act of climbing or rising
assent	n./v.	an acceptance of an idea as true; to give permission
accept	v.	to agree, approve, or receive
access	v./n.	to make or find available; a way of approach
except	v./prep.	to exclude from
acute	adj.	severe, critical, beginning suddenly
chronic	adj.	continuing over a long time
adverse	adj.	hostile, unfavorable, difficult
averse (to)	adj.	opposed
advice	n.	opinion or counsel
advise	v.	to give counsel or advice

Word	Part of Speech	Description or Meaning
affect	n./v.	the emotional domain; to influence
effect	n./v.	the result; to make happen
aggravate	v.	to make worse
annoy	v.	to irritate
a lot	adv./adj.	many
allot	v.	to distribute; to assign in portions
alott	n.	a one-humped camel
allude	v.	to refer to indirectly
elude	v.	to escape
refer	v.	to mention directly
allusion	n.	an indirect reference
illusion	n.	a false impression or misleading appearance
altar	n.	a holy table used for worship
alter	v.	to change

Word	Part of Speech	Description or Meaning
among	prep.	shows relationship with three or more
between	prep.	shows relationship with two
amount	n.	used for quantities or masses that are measured, not counted
number	n.	used for quantities that are counted, not measured
and	conj.	shows equal, additional relationship
but	conj.	shows that the latter statement discounts or minimizes the first statement
or	conj.	shows that only one of the choices will remain
plus	prep./adj.	a mathematical expression for the addition operation; a positive addition, credit

Word	Part of Speech	Description or Meaning
angel	n.	a celestial being
angle	v./n.	to slant toward, or to fish; a point of view, or the difference in the direction of two intersecting lines as measured by degrees, minutes, and seconds
anterior	adj.	toward the front, top, or head in anatomy
posterior	adj.	toward the back, bottom, or rear in anatomy
anxious	adj.	nervous
eager	adj.	excited with anticipation
are	v.	the present plural form of *to be*
hour	n.	sixty minutes
our	pron.	the first person plural possessive pronoun that matches *we* and *us*
as	prep.	shows comparisons and introduces a clause or phrase
like	adj./prep	sameness or introduces a prepositional phrase

Appendix C: Usage Lists

Word	Part of Speech	Description or Meaning
assure	v.	to make certain or to tell as a fact to someone
ensure	v.	to promise
insure	v.	to guarantee with money or insurance
bad	adj.	not good; used after an auxiliary or helping verb
badly	adv.	not good; used after an action verb
balance	n./v.	maintaining equillibrium; to make a financial reconciliation
remainder	n./adj.	a mathematical term for a part that is left over after the operation
baring	v.	uncovering
barring	v.	putting up a barrier
bearing	v.	carrying
Bering	n.	part of the Pacific Ocean and the strait that divides America from Asia

Word	Part of Speech	Description or Meaning
berth	n.	a seat or a sleeping area
birth	n.	the act of having life by being born
beside	prep.	next to, adjacent
besides	prep.	in addition to, other than
best	adj.	the most excellent
better	adj.	somewhat excellent
good	adj.	a fine quality, yet less than excellent
well	adj./adv.	healthy; abundantly or properly
board	n.	a group of people who govern or a wooden slab
bored	v./adj.	to have made a hole; dulled interest and attention
born	v.	to have been given life through birth
borne	v.	past participle form of *bear*
bourn	v.	British spelling for having given birth

Word	Part of Speech	Description or Meaning
borrow	v.	to take with the intent of returning
lend	v.	to offer something of value temporarily
loan	n.	the item that is temporarily given away to be returned later with an added bonus
bring	v.	to carry something toward the speaker
carry	v.	to lift and hold something while moving it
take	v.	to carry something away from the speaker
can	v.	to express the ability to do something
may	v.	to express the permission or possibility to do something
canvas	n.	stiff material that tailors and artists use
canvass	n./v.	the act of seeking votes; to seek votes or examine for accuracy

Word	Part of Speech	Description or Meaning
capital	n./adj.	the city of a central government, money; upper case print
capitol	n.	the central building for a government
carat	n.	the weight of a precious or semiprecious stone
caret	n.	a copyeditor's mark showing an insertion
carrot	n.	a root vegetable
cement	n./v.	the powder that forms an adhesive when mixed with sand, gravel, and water; to join
concrete	n./adj.	the mix of cement with other ingredients to create a solid construction material; not abstract and experienced through the body's senses
chord	n.	a set of musical notes
cord	n.	a line for pulling or tying

Word	Part of Speech	Description or Meaning
cite	v.	to say or give facts
sight	n./v.	something seen with the eyes; to observe
site	n.	a location
coarse	adj.	rough texture, harsh
course	n.	a study unit of curriculum; a facility that can be mapped
collaboration	n.	the act of agreeing
collusion	n.	the act of conspiring secretly and dishonestly
collage	n.	a work of art made from many separate pieces
college	n.	an institution of higher learning
compare (to)	v.	shows similarities
compare (with)	v.	shows similarities and differences
comparison	n.	shows similarities only or both similarities and differences
contrast	n./v.	shows differences only

Word	Part of Speech	Description or Meaning
complement	n.	something that is completed or compatible
compliment	n.	praise or a gift
confidant	n.	a trusted person
confident	adj.	having trust
conscience	n.	the inner ethical sense
conscious	adj.	deliberate, aware, awake
consequently	adv.	as a result of
subsequently	adv.	following after or later
continually	adv.	frequently repeated with intervals
continuously	adv.	always going without stop
core	n./v.	the center; to remove the inside pit or center
corps	n.	a tight group
corpse	n.	a dead body

Word	Part of Speech	Description or Meaning
costume	n.	special clothes for an occasion
custom	n.	a tradition
council	n.	a body or organization created to advise or legislate
counsel	n./v.	a legal adviser or the advice resulting from consultation; to advise or consult
cymbal	n.	a percussion instrument in music
simple	adj.	not complex
symbol	n.	something that represents something else
dairy	n.	a place where milk products are sold or made
diary	n.	a daily journal
dire	adj.	terrible, dreadful

Word	Part of Speech	Description or Meaning
data	n.	either plural or singular, meaning evidence or information
datum	n.	formerly the singular of *data;* the beginning measure for a survey
decent	adj.	respectable
descent	n.	a downward movement
de-scent	v.	to remove the scent gland
dissent	n./v.	disagreement; to disagree, refuse, or oppose
deductive	adj.	logic moving from the specific facts or details to the general principle
inductive	adj.	logic moving from the general principle to the specific facts or details
deprave	v.	to corrupt or pervert
deprive	v.	to withhod or take away something wanted or needed

Word	Part of Speech	Description or Meaning
deprecate	v.	to express disapproval of something
depreciate	v.	to diminish the value of something
despite	prep.	notwithstanding, regardless of
inspite	prep.	a nonstandard form of *despite* that is gaining popularity
in spite (of)	prep.	regardless of
desert	n./v.	a barren, arid land; to leave without warning or permission
dessert	n.	usually a sweet food served after a meal
device	n.	an object or tool
devise	v.	to create

Word	Part of Speech	Description or Meaning
diagnosis	n.	the identification of a disease or problem from its symptoms
prescription	n.	the medical treatment or plan for a disease, or a professional plan for treating a problem
prognosis	n.	an assessment of the probable course of a disease or problem and the chances of recovery
different from	prep.	the formal choice for contrast
different than	prep.	the nonstandard, popular choice for contrast
digit	n.	any one number from zero to nine; a finger or toe
number	n./v.	a word or symbol to show quantity or sequence; to count
numeral	n.	the symbol or group of symbols for a number, such as Roman or Arabic numerals

Word	Part of Speech	Description or Meaning
discriminate	v.	to make distinctions and judgments
prejudice	n./v.	a preconceived opinion; to impair the validity of something
prejudiced	adj.	having a preconceived opinion
disinterested	adj.	neutral, uninvolved
uninterested	adj.	bored, not interested
dual	adj.	having two parts, double
duel	n./v.	a fight, arranged and conducted according to a code of honor; to fight under such a code
elicit	v.	to draw out or invite
illicit	adj.	illegal, prohibited
emigrant	n.	a person who leaves his or her own country
immigrant	n.	a person who enters another country

Word	Part of Speech	Description or Meaning
eminent	adj.	distinguished, prominent
imminent	adj.	prediction of something happening soon
emphasize	v.	to show importance
stress	n./v.	a substandard, popular version of *distress* and/or *eustress;* to accent or emphasize
eave	n.	an overhang constructed from the lower edge of a roof on a building
eve	n.	early night or evening; the day before a special day
farther	adv.	shows physical distance
further	adv.	shows intellectual distance
fewer	adv.	used with count nouns (things that can be counted)
less	adj./adv.	used with noncount nouns (amounts or quantities that are measured)

Word	Part of Speech	Description or Meaning
former	adj./n.	the first of two or more
latter	adj./n.	the last of two or more
forth	n.	a forward movement in time or distance
fourth	n./adj.	the one after the third; being the one after the third
from	prep.	indicating outward movement, distiction, place of origin, separation, cause, source, or deprivation
since	adv./prep.	at some point in the past and now; because, after
gamble	v.	to bet, to play a game for money or gain
gambol	n./v.	playful leaping; to leap about
holy	adj.	sacred, pure, spiritual
holly	n.	a prickly-leafed green plant
holistic	adj.	viewing a complete approach of the whole
wholly	adv.	completely

Word	Part of Speech	Description or Meaning
I	pron.	first person singular, subjective case; performs the action or existence
me	pron.	first person singular, objective case; receives the action in the sentence
myself	pron.	first person singular, emphatic or reflective; refers to *I* in the same sentence
if	conj.	showing a conditional situation, often at the beginning of a sentence
whether	conj.	a formal choice for a conditional situation, used after the verb
imply	v.	to suggest indirectly
infer	v.	to examine evidence and draw a conclusion
incredible	adj.	unbelievable, amazing
incredulous	adj.	unwilling to believe, doubtful

Word	Part of Speech	Description or Meaning
it's	contr.	it is
its	pron.	possessive, third-person singular; follows the pattern of *hers, his, theirs, ours, yours*
instance	n	one time
instants	n.	moments or seconds
lay	v.	past tense of *lie* or present tense meaning to place something; used with an object
lie	v.	to recline or to tell a falsehood
lectern	n.	a raised desk with a sloping top for a speaker's papers
podium	n.	the riser or stage that a speaker stands on
loose	adj.	not tight, having slack
lose	v.	to misplace or be defeated
majority	n.	more than half of a group
plurality	n.	the largest part of a group when there is no majority

Word	Part of Speech	Description or Meaning
meat	n.	the flesh of animals used for food
meet	n./v.	a gathering, as for a sporting event; to become acquainted or gather
mete	v.	to distribute or hand out
medal	n.	a small, flat piece of metal used to commemorate an event
metal	n.	an element, or a compound or alloy of such an element that conducts heat and electricity
moot	adj.	lacking power or relevance
mute	adj./n.	being unable to talk; a person who is unable to talk
moral	n.	a lesson
morale	n.	state of mind
morning	n.	the time of day after dawn and before noon
mourning	n./v.	the grief period after a death; grieving, feeling sorrow

Word	Part of Speech	Description or Meaning
oar	n/v.	a paddle used to propel or steer a boat; to propel, steer, or row
or	conj.	a word that links ideas, things, or people to show only one will be chosen from the group; creates an alternative
ore	n.	a valuable mineral containing metals and other substances
passed	v.	past tense of *pass;* to go around or beyond
past	n./adj.	prior to the present tense
percent	n.	an exact amount of a whole
percentage	n.	an unknown amount of the whole
personal	adj.	private, individual
personnel	n.	office or institution staff

Word	Part of Speech	Description or Meaning
perspective	n.	an evaluation and interpretation of events based on a point of view, or the appearance of objects with respect to distance, position, and importance
prospective	adj.	expected to become
prospectus	n.	a publication containing information such as an annual business report
plain	n./adj.	a large, open area of land; simple, unembellished, easy to understand
plan	n./v.	the procedure or system of action; to organize or arrange
plane	n./v.	a short term for an airplane, a level surface, or a carpenter's tool; to level a surface with a carpenter's tool
precede	v.	to go before
proceed	v.	to move forward
proceeds	n.	money acquired from an event

Word	Part of Speech	Description or Meaning
precedence	n.	the act, right, or privilege of going before, usually according to rank or status
precedents	n.	the cases that have been decided earlier and that influence later cases
presence	n.	the existence of something here now
presents	n./v.	gifts; to announce or award another
principal	n./adj.	the head of an organization or money applied to an asset; the most important
principle	n.	an idea
profit	n./v.	a personal or financial gain; to gain or benefit from
prophet	n.	a person who teaches, preaches, predicts, and counsels

Word	Part of Speech	Description or Meaning
property	n.	real estate or things owned
propriety	n.	correctness or suitability
proprietary	adj.	relating to ownership or the right of ownership
proprietaries	n.	a body of owners
prophecy	n.	the lesson, sermon, prediction, or advice of a prophet
prophesy	v.	to give a lesson, sermon, prediction, or advice of a prophet
prostate	n.	the male sex gland located at the neck of the bladder
prostrate	v./adj.	to cast to the ground face downward; lying face downward with body extended in exhaustion or defeat
pupil	n.	a learner in elementary school
student	n.	a learner in high school or college

Word	Part of Speech	Description or Meaning
quiet	n./adj.	silence; silent
quit	v.	to stop
quite	adj.	more than the typical
rain	n./v.	wet precipitation dropping from the clouds; to fall as rain
reign	n./v.	the power of a monarch or the period of office; to hold royal office
rein	n.	one of the two leather straps used to control an animal
reek	v.	to have a foul smell or smoke, to have a lot in abundance
wreak	v.	to inflict or give full force to
right	n.	the opposite of left; correct; a quality attributed with consent
rite	n.	a ritual
write	v.	to compose with letters and words

Word	Part of Speech	Description or Meaning
ring	n./v.	a circle or piece of jewelry for the finger; to sound out, to telephone
wring	v.	to squeeze and twist, as in removing water from fabric
sat	v.	past tense of *sit*
set	v.	to put something down; used with an object
sit	v.	to take a seat
shone	v.	past participle of *shine*
shown	v.	past participle of *show*
sold	v./adj.	past tense of *sell*; to have exchanged for payment
sole	n.	a kind of fish; the bottom of a shoe
soul	n.	the spirit
staid	adj.	set in steady habits, well balanced yet dull
stayed	v.	past tense of *stay*

Word	Part of Speech	Description or Meaning
stake	n.	a spike or an investment
steak	n.	a special cut of beef
stationary	adj.	still, unmoving
stationery	n.	writing paper used for correspondence
steal	v.	to take what is not yours
steel	n.	an alloy of iron and carbon
steer	n./v.	a young castrated bull; to direct the course of
stir	v.	to mix
than	conj.	shows comparison
then	adv.	shows time
that	pron.	shows a restrictive clause that is essential to the meaning of the sentence
which	pron.	shows a nonrestrictive meaning that merely supplements, but does not change, the meaning of the sentence

Word	Part of Speech	Description or Meaning
their	pron.	possessive, third person plural form showing belongingness
there	pron./adv.	used to begin a sentence to avoid the subject first; a place away from the speaker
they're	contr.	they are
to	prep./adv.	shows relationship or an infinitive fixed or fastened; becoming conscious, as in *coming to*
too	adv.	also; shows extreme
two	adj./n.	the number after one and before three
use	v.	to employ something; to put into action or service
utilize	v.	to convert to use; to be creative with actual resources at hand
vain	adj.	conscious
vane	n.	a weather device that shows the direction of the wind
vein	n.	a vessel that carries blood away from the heart; a vessel that carries nutrients in plants

Word	Part of Speech	Description or Meaning
villain	n.	a wicked character or person capable of vile deeds
villein	n.	a workman bound in his service to his feudal lord or estate
wait	n./v.	a period of waiting; to stay until something happens or someone arrives
weight	n.	the measurement of ounces and pounds
waste	n./v.	garbage or stuff thrown away; to throw away or use partially
weak	adj.	not strong
week	n.	seven days
weather	n.	atmospheric conditions of climate
wether	n.	a castrated male sheep
whether	conj.	a formal choice for a conditional situation, used after the verb

Word	Part of Speech	Description or Meaning
who	pron.	refers to a person in the subjective case; replaces *I, he, she,* or *they*
whom	pron.	refers to a person in the objective case; replaces *me, him, her,* or *them*
who's	contr.	who is, who has
whose	pron.	belongs to the person referred to as who
yore	n.	long ago
your	pron.	possessive form of *you*
you're	contr.	you are

Although many of these meanings are subtle, the excellent writers and proofreaders recognize these words on sight. Your readers will thank you!

Outdated Expressions

Avoid	Use
at this point in time	now
at this date	now
for the purpose of	to

Avoid	Use
in order to	to
in the event that	if
due to the fact that	because
for the reason that	because
inasmuch as	because
in the final analysis	finally
until such time as	until
pertaining to	about
subsequent to	after
transpire	happen
try to line up a meeting	arrange a meeting
I would suggest that	please
feel free to call	call me if . . .
don't hesitate to call	call me if . . .
please be advised that	(delete)
our situation is such that	(delete)
forward it on to me	send it to me
enclosed please find	I've enclosed
we are in receipt of	we have received
we acknowledge receipt of	thank you for your . . .
per your request	as you asked
in accordance to your request	as you requested

Avoid	*Use*
under separate cover	we're sending it to you by regular mail
pursuant to	according to
pursuant to your order	following your instructions
we are cognizant that	we know (that)
it is with deep regret	I'm sorry
we take pleasure	we are happy
everyone . . . he	people . . . they
To whom it may concern	Dear Authority (Director, President)
Dear Sir or Madam	Dear (name or title)
thank you in advance	I'd appreciate your help
Very sincerely yours	Sincerely
downsizing, right-sizing, reengineering	changing
facilitate	make easy
utilize	use

Photocopy this list for your writers so they can update their expressions before you review their writing. It'll save everyone time and embarrassment.

Other expressions are equally as distracting as outdated terms. The following section lists other words the proofreader should know.

Empty Words

Word(s)	*Reason to Avoid or Delete*
affect, effect	often confused
am, is, are, was, were	forms of *to be*
anxious	confused with *eager*
between	confused with *among*
by	often used to complete the passive voice for indirect communication
Dear Sir	use only if the salutation is directed toward a specific man
except	confused with *accept*
have, has, had	forms of *to have*
here, it, there	weak leads in sentences that delay the image of stronger, better sentence embedded in the words that follow
I believe, I think	use only for emphasis or clarification, not as an empty introduction that diffuses the audience's attention
in spite	a nonstandard form of *despite*
interesting	too general to be helpful
it, they, you	vague when undefined or when shifted without clear transitions
nice	too vague to be helpful

Word(s)	Reason to Avoid or Delete
really, so, too, very	overused words that diffuse the audience's attention
thing	too vague to be helpful
utilize	a pretentious, faddish misuse of *use*

Simplifying usually makes a sentence sound stronger and more persuasive. Ask the writer to judge the difference.

Killer Words

Word(s)	Reason for Reconsidering
always, never	extremes; overstatements that are hard to prove
blame, error, failure, fault, mistake, terminate	allow an unproductive focus
but	discounts the statement that precedes it
can't, don't	create a negative focus
claim	the tone sounds as if someone is lying or deceiving someone else
hisself, irregardless, theirself	illiterate terms
ladies, madam	dated expressions that may be perceived as condescending

Word(s)	Reason for Reconsidering
no, not, never	negatives that elicit negative thinking and additional mental effort to process
try	provides an inherent excuse for failure or noncompliance

Work as a team with the writer to determine the best choices for substitutions above. The writer will appreciate your concern, and the reader will enjoy a better experience.

Persuasive Words

A study at Yale University determined that the most persuasive words in the American English language are those listed below:

you	money
save	new
easy	free
guarantee	love
discovery	results
health	proven

When you read any of these words, check to make sure the writer can "back them up." The reader can be influenced by the words alone, but not for long unless the writer means them.

Another way to influence a reader is with action-oriented words. The proofreader may recommend the next list to the staff writers.

Action Words

Action-oriented words are easier for a reader to remember because they are processed through the senses. Some examples follow.

accomplish	counsel
achieve	create
act	decrease
administer	design
advise	develop
agree	devise
analyze	direct
assist	enlarge
attain	ensure
benefit	establish
build	evaluate
call	expand
communicate	file
complete	gain
conduct	generate
construct	guide
control	hear
coordinate	implement

improve	reduce
increase	research
initiate	resolve
invent	satisfy
invite	see
lead	select
learn	sell
listen	serve
maintain	show
make	solve
manage	speak
negotiate	start
order	state
organize	succeed
originate	survey
plan	teach
please	thank
prepare	train
produce	type
profit	use
raise	value
recommend	write
record	yield

Writers, use action words to capture your reader's attention as you add the promise of credibility to your documents. Proofreaders, use these words to capture your writer's attention while discussing ways to improve the document. Although offering these words is part of the editing function, a good proofreader can always suggest alternatives that the reader may appreciate.

Appendix D: Transitions

Transitions are the words and phrases that help readers follow the writer's thinking from one idea to the next. They make the message flow. Transitions protect the reader from whiplash and add polish to persuasiveness. Each acts as a signal for the direction and development of ideas. The proofreader may advise the writer to insert a word or a phrase to create a smooth connection between ideas. Some functions and samples of transitions appear below.

- **To show that what follows is extra or supplementary**

again	first	moreover
also	furthermore	next
and	in addition	nor
besides	indeed	or
finally	in fact	second

- **To show a contradiction, antithesis, or contrast**

although	however	though
and yet	nevertheless	whereas
but	nonetheless	yet
despite this fact	notwithstanding	
even so	still	

- **To show similarity**

in much the same manner	once again	similarly
likewise	once more	

- **To show a result of a preceding cause**

accordingly	consequently	on the whole
all in all	finally	so
and so	for this reason	therefore
and this is why	hence	thus
as a consequence	in conclusion	
as a result	in summary	

- **To show anticipation**

as a matter of fact	naturally	surely
for that matter	of course	to be expected
it follows that		

- **To show reasons**

  because   for   since

- **To show concessions**

  certainly   no doubt that   to be certain

  doubtless   of course   to be sure

  granted that

- **To show qualifications**

  especially   in particular   specifically

  frequently   occasionally   usually

  in general   often

- **To show restrictions**

  if provided   lest   unless

  in case   provided   when

- **To show example**

  for example   in the same way   similarly

  for instance   likewise   to illustrate

- **To show emphasis**

  again   indeed

  in any case   most importantly

- **To show temporal relationship**

afterwards	immediately	soon after
at last	in the meantime	subsequently
at length	later	the next time
at that moment	meanwhile	then
before	presently	thereafter
beforehand	previously	when
by that time	shortly	while
earlier	simultaneously	within the hour
following this	spontaneously	
from then on	soon	

- **To show spatial relationship**

above	between	on the perimeter
adjacent to	beyond	straight ahead
approximately a foot away	diagonally	to the east
at that altitude	horizontally	to the left
at the center	in the next space	vertically
below	next to this	
beside	on the edge	

- **To show summary**

all in all	in conclusion	to summarize
altogether this means	in summary	what this means is
in brief	therefore	

- **To show reference**

another	she	who
anything	someone	whom
everybody	that	whose
he	they	you
it	we	
other	which	

Appendix E: Type Guide and Specifications

Attention to detail is the sign of an excellent proofreader. Knowing the kinds, sizes, and styles of the fonts requested or required for a document is not enough; the proofreader must check for them. This guide will help in that process.

Sample Fonts

Chicago

Geneva

Monaco

New York

Courier

Helvetica

Palatino

Times Roman

Common Styles

Normal (text weight)	*Boldface*	*Italic*
Helvetica	**Helvetica**	*Helvetica*
Times Roman	**Times Roman**	*Times Roman*
Courier	**Courier**	*Courier*

189

Underline	Strike Through
Helvetica	~~Helvetica~~
Times Roman	~~Times Roman~~
Courier	~~Courier~~

Common Sizes in Points

6	Helvetica	Times Roman	Courier
8	Helvetica	Times Roman	Courier
9	Helvetica	Times Roman	Courier
10	Helvetica	Times Roman	Courier
12	Helvetica	Times Roman	Courier
14	Helvetica	Times Roman	Courier
18	Helvetica	Times Roman	Courier
24	Helveti	Times Ro	Courie
30	Helve	Times	Couri

36	Helv	Times	Cour
48	Hel	Tim	Cou
60	He	Tim	Co
72	He	Ti	Co
96	HeTic		

Helvetica is a sans serif type, good for titles and headings. Sans serif fonts give a clean, sharp image.

Times Roman is an excellent serifed choice for text, allowing the reader's eyes to flow easily from one letter to the next, thus making reading faster than with a sans serif font.

```
Courier in 12-point type or larger is
a fine choice for fax transmittals
because it's large enough to be clear
and many of the early machines were
designed to carry this font.
```

You may need to make recommendations regarding type specifications because this material falls into the visual communication category, which is the first impression the reader will have about the document. Warn the writer to use only three or four different visual components on a page to avoid overwhelming the reader.

You have now reached the end of *Proof Positive,* the text, and are ready to begin positive proofreading, the task. Use this book as a reference. Mark it, tab it—make it into a map to guide your language vehicle and the reader-passenger through the writer's territory. May your ride be smooth!

Available From SkillPath Publications

Self-Study Sourcebooks

Climbing the Corporate Ladder: What You Need to Know and Do to Be a Promotable Person *by Barbara Pachter and Marjorie Brody*

Coping With Supervisory Nightmares: 12 Common Nightmares of Leadership and What You Can Do About Them *by Michael and Deborah Singer Dobson*

Discovering Your Purpose *by Ivy Haley*

Going for the Gold: Winning the Gold Medal for Financial Independence *by Lesley D. Bissett, CFP*

The Innovative Secretary *by Marlene Caroselli, Ed.D.*

Mastering the Art of Communication: Your Keys to Developing a More Effective Personal Style *by Michelle Fairfield Poley*

Organized for Success! 95 Tips for Taking Control of Your Time, Your Space, and Your Life *by Nanci McGraw*

P.E.R.S.U.A.D.E.: Communication Strategies That Move People to Action *by Marlene Caroselli, Ed.D.*

Productivity Power: 250 Great Ideas for Being More Productive *by Jim Temme*

Promoting Yourself: 50 Ways to Increase Your Prestige, Power, and Paycheck *by Marlene Caroselli, Ed.D.*

Risk-Taking: 50 Ways to Turn Risks Into Rewards *by Marlene Caroselli, Ed.D. and David Harris*

Stress Control: How You Can Find Relief From Life's Daily Stress *by Steve Bell*

The Technical Writer's Guide *by Robert McGraw*

Total Quality Customer Service: How to Make It Your Way of Life *by Jim Temme*

Write It Right! A Guide for Clear and Correct Writing *by Richard Andersen and Helene Hinis*

Handbooks

The ABC's of Empowered Teams: Building Blocks for Success *by Mark Towers*

Assert Yourself! Developing Power-Packed Communication Skills to Make Your Points Clearly, Confidently, and Persuasively *by Lisa Contini*

Breaking the Ice: How to Improve Your On-the-Spot Communication Skills *by Deborah Shouse*

The Care and Keeping of Customers: A Treasury of Facts, Tips, and Proven Techniques for Keeping Your Customers Coming BACK! *by Roy Lantz*

Challenging Change: Five Steps for Dealing With Change *by Holly DeForest and Mary Steinberg*

Dynamic Delegation: A Manager's Guide for Active Empowerment *by Mark Towers*

Every Woman's Guide to Career Success *by Denise M. Dudley*

Great Openings and Closings: 28 Ways to Launch and Land Your Presentations With Punch, Power, and Pizazz *by Mari Pat Varga*

Hiring and Firing: What Every Manager Needs to Know *by Marlene Caroselli, Ed.D. with Laura Wyeth, Ms.Ed.*

How to Be a More Effective Group Communicator: Finding Your Role and Boosting Your Confidence in Group Situations *by Deborah Shouse*

How to Deal With Difficult People *by Paul Friedman*

Learning to Laugh at Work: The Power of Humor in the Workplace *by Robert McGraw*

Making Your Mark: How to Develop a Personal Marketing Plan for Becoming More Visible and More Appreciated at Work *by Deborah Shouse*

Meetings That Work *by Marlene Caroselli, Ed.D.*

The Mentoring Advantage: How to Help Your Career Soar to New Heights *by Pam Grout*

Minding Your Business Manners: Etiquette Tips for Presenting Yourself Professionally in Every Business Situation *by Marjorie Brody and Barbara Pachter*

Misspeller's Guide *by Joel and Ruth Schroeder*

Motivation in the Workplace: How to Motivate Workers to Peak Performance and Productivity *by Barbara Fielder*

NameTags Plus: Games You Can Play When People Don't Know What to Say *by Deborah Shouse*

Networking: How to Creatively Tap Your People Resources *by Colleen Clarke*

New & Improved! 25 Ways to Be More Creative and More Effective *by Pam Grout*

Power Write! A Practical Guide to Words That Work *by Helene Hinis*

Putting Anger to Work For You! *by Ruth and Joel Schroeder*

Reinventing Your Self: 28 Strategies for Coping With Change *by Mark Towers*

Saying "No" to Negativity: How to Manage Negativity in Yourself, Your Boss, and Your Co-Workers *by Zoie Kaye*

The Supervisor's Guide: The Everyday Guide to Coordinating People and Tasks *by Jerry Brown and Denise Dudley, Ph.D.*

Taking Charge: A Personal Guide to Managing Projects and Priorities *by Michal E. Feder*

Treasure Hunt: 10 Stepping Stones to a New and More Confident You! *by Pam Grout*

A Winning Attitude: How to Develop Your Most Important Asset! *by Michelle Fairfield Poley*

For more information, call 1-800-873-7545.

Notes

Notes